CONTENTS

Faith, Forgiveness, & Fibromyalgia

Nance Fabretti

ISBN 978-1-0980-1102-4 (paperback)
ISBN 978-1-0980-1103-1 (digital)

Cover art provided by Naturally Inspired Photography.
https://photosbyjennylee.wixsite.com/naturallyinspired
naturallyinspiredphotograpy@gmail.com

Christian Faith Publishing, Inc.
832 Park Avenue
Meadville, PA 16335
www.christianfaithpublishing.com

Printed in the United States of America

A chronicle of God's amazing power and marvelous works. To "declare his glory among the nations, His marvelous deeds among all peoples" (1 Chronicles 16:24).

To my favorite Sister in law—

I pray the content of this book showcases the incredible and intimate God who whispers to you in the still of the day, "You are my Beloved."

"Let the beloved of the Lord rest secure in him, for he shields him all day long, and the one the Lord loves rests between his shoulders" (Deuteronomy 33:12).

I hope the content of this book draws you closer to Our Heavenly Father —

Love
Nance Fabetti

To my pastor, Robert Larson, and his wife, my dear friend, Angela, who have taught the Word of God faithfully and with tenacity. They have taught the application of the Word in real life, which is so important if we are to live it out in this world and prepare for eternity. I am who I am today because of their faithfulness, friendship, and ability to speak the truth in love and to pour the truths of scripture into my life so that I may do the same for others.

It is my desire to be a conduit of God's love, care, and keeping a lifelike example of the Miraculous God, who delivers, heals, and makes whole. I wish to reach people with the transforming Word of God so that they will know the Creator of the universe who loves them and has a purpose and plan for their lives. Victorious lives! Not a this-is-the-best-I-can-do life, but a life with trials that build character and creates an opportunity for the miraculous works of God. This life is described in Colossians 3:16 as one in which the Word dwells richly, transforming a heap of ashes into something incredibly beautiful.

Thank you, Pastor Bob and Angela!

PREFACE

In Deuteronomy 11:1–7, God speaks to the Israelites after their Exodus out of Egypt:

> Love the Lord your God and keep his require-
> ments, his decrees, his laws and his commands
> always. Remember today that your children were
> not the ones who saw and experienced the dis-
> cipline of the Lord your God: his majesty, his
> mighty hand, his outstretched arm; the signs he
> performed and the things he did in the heart of
> Egypt, both to Pharaoh, king of Egypt and to his
> whole country; what he did to the Egyptian army,
> to its horses and chariots, how he overwhelmed
> them with the waters of the Red Sea and how the
> Lord brought lasting ruin on them. It was not
> your children who saw what he did for you in the
> wilderness. But it was your own eyes that saw all
> these great things the Lord has done.

So here we are told that our children may not have seen or were too young to remember the times when God answered prayer; there-fore, we need to tell them.

Deuteronomy 11:18–20 goes on to say,

> Fix these words of mine in your hearts and
> minds; tie them as symbols on your hands and

bind them on your foreheads. Teach them to your children, talking about them when you sit at home and when you walk along the road, when you lie down and when you get up. Write them on the doorframes of your houses and on your gates, so that your days and the days of your children may be many in the land the Lord swore to give your ancestors, as many as the days that the heavens are above the earth.

God is expressing to the Israelites and the next generations of believers (us) the importance of telling our children the marvelous word and works of God. To speak about them throughout our day when we lie down and when we get up, when we sit and when we walk along the road. In our going out and our coming in, we see them on the doorposts and the gates. God's works are marvelous! Therefore, we need to tell others about them, especially to the generations that follow.

The times when we have experienced a work of God in our lives are monumental times or memorials. God teaches us the importance of these memorials in Joshua chapters 3 and 4:

The Israelites were getting ready to cross the Jordan River.

Now the Jordan is at flood stage all during harvest. Yet as soon as the priests who carried the ark reached the Jordan and their feet touched the water's edge, the water from upstream stopped flowing. It piled up in a heap a great distance away, while the water flowing down was completely cut off. The priests who carried the ark of the covenant of the Lord stopped in the middle of the Jordan and stood on dry ground, while all Israel passed by until the whole nation had completed the crossing on dry ground.

Then the Lord said to Joshua, "Choose twelve men from among the people, one from each tribe, and tell them to take up twelve stones from the middle of the Jordan, from right where the priests are standing, and carry them over with you and put them down at the place where you stay tonight.

"This is to serve as a sign among you. In the future, when your children ask you, 'What do these stones mean?' tell them that the flow of the Jordan was cut off before the ark of the covenant of the Lord. These stones are to be a memorial to the people of Israel forever."

The Lord has taught me so much in the thirty-plus years that I have served Him. When I read His Word, I can tell you the specific times in my life and the circumstances surrounding my application of that particular verse and its outcome. Each chapter, I have written in this book is a memorial to tell of God's faithfulness, miracles, and works so as never to forget his goodness, mercy, and grace. He impressed on me several years ago to write, and I am finally obediently doing so.

God has taken this heap of ashes called my life, and He is making something beautiful. At one time, all I ever wanted was to know love and to be loved. God has demonstrated His love toward me. He has performed so many miracles in my life. My identity is now found in who He says I am. It is beneficial for my story to be told, for truly it is His story.

It is my desire that reading this book will instill hope in you. The hope that comes from knowing the One True God, the Lover of your soul, the One who fights for you, the Creator of the universe, and so much more. He is alive and well and cares deeply for you. He wants you to know that He has a plan and a purpose for your life. He wants to lead and direct you to bring about a quality of life that you could never experience without Him.

I pray the content of this book showcases that incredible and intimate God who whispers to you in the still of the day, "You are my beloved."

"Let the beloved of the Lord rest secure in him, for he shields him all day long, and the one the Lord loves rests between his shoulders" (Deuteronomy 33:12).

INTRODUCTION

W hen my children were young, three and six, I gave my whole heart to Jesus and began being discipled but did not have a home church. The kids and I had visited a few churches, and I desired to settle in long term somewhere.

I asked God to please show me where my children and I should attend. With all my heart, I wanted a church where I could dig deep into the Word of God and mature, and my children could grow in the truth of the scriptures.

The people who were discipling me said they had heard of a church that was solid in the Word of God. I agreed to go to a Bible study that night, but I was thinking this would be the last time I would visit a church until the Lord showed me my home church.

As I walked into the first floor chapel, the place felt so familiar. We sat down, and the seat I sat in, I had seen before. Then I noticed a column in the midst of the room. As I sat there, I remembered a recent dream in which I was in this very place. The dream became so vivid in my mind. Bible study was great, and at the end, some people introduced themselves to us. One gentleman came toward me to say hello, and that confirmed it all. This man was in my dream! I saw this room, the seat that I sat in, and that column. The final detail was this young man, Tim.

I processed what occurred for a little while, telling no one.

The Lord impressed on me that I had cried out to him, and he heard me. This will be my home church. If you prayed, and then the Lord gave you a dream and showed you where he was sending you, and then you physically found yourself in that very place, you might want to shout it from the rooftops, right? But I didn't, maybe because it seemed outlandish. Isn't it funny that we pray expecting God to answer, and when He does, it seems so unbelievable. So instead, I pondered this in my heart for a long time. In Luke 2, scripture states that, "Mary treasured up all these things and pondered them in her heart." I felt like Mary. This wonderful thing God has shown me and done for me made me feel so very special. He heard my prayer and gave me a dream to solidify what I would experience upon visiting this church. The people who were discipling me and brought me to this church determined that they were not going back. I knew this was the place that my Heavenly Father was sending me. Those people cut ties with me since I chose not to follow their direction. It was bittersweet since they had taken time to teach me about the scriptures, and I was very appreciative; however, I needed to follow the Lord's leading. This would set the stage for future times when I would have to make decisions for the Lord amongst well-meaning voices telling me to do otherwise.

I have attended Crossroads Church of God ever since and have grown and flourished under the pastorship of Robert Larson and his beautiful wife, Angela.

CHAPTER 1

Let Me Introduce Myself

I grew up in a small town. One of my fondest memories is of my dad playing the accordion at night while my sister and I had a pillow fight in our bedroom. Our bedroom was situated at the back of the house, and there was an enclosed porch at the front of the house with a long corridor and a kitchen in between. In the evening after putting us to bed, my dad would take out his accordion, settle down in the enclosed porch, and play. Meanwhile, down the hall in the bedroom, my sister and I would stand at the end of our beds and swat each other in the head with our pillows as soon as we heard the music. If the accordion stopped playing, we would freeze. When the music began playing, we would begin swatting.

If the music stopped, we would freeze in whatever position we were in at the time. Every now and then, the music would stop for a little while longer. *Uh oh, do you hear steps? He's coming!* We would dive into our respective beds and act as though we had been slumbering for hours. His feet would stop at the threshold of our bedroom—stillness, quiet—then a step forward, and he would lean in to see our faces. I could never wipe the grin off of my face so I would turn toward the wall; it was all I could do not to let out a giggle.

Well, those days ended with the divorce. The next thing I knew, we were moving to a new place in the same small town, and we were introduced to our new stepdad, Bill. Bill liked to smoke cherry-flavored Erik cigars, especially when taking a drive, but he never rolled the windows down in the car. He tried to be the man in my life, but truly, no one takes the place of your dad.

A few years went by, and we were moving to a city where Bill worked. It was pretty cool at first, an apartment building with an elevator, next to a McDonald's restaurant and Dunkin Donuts. I met kids who lived in the apartment buildings and hung out. We played hide and go seek in the backyard, the card game Spit in the hallways, and we rode the elevator up and down four floors.

My mom and Bill divorced, and we moved numerous times throughout this city over the next several years. With the moves came new schools and new friends. My mom worked really hard to make a life for us, but she was struggling with a great deal of "baggage." Her dad drowned when she was eighteen years old, and as a result, her mom began to drink heavily. I'm told that she would bring my mom along to the bars for company. It is my understanding that this is how my mom developed a taste for alcohol, which would eventually tear her life apart.

We all come with some sort of baggage. I always wanted to have a family like the Brady Bunch. You know, the kind of family that has a level-headed hard-working dad, and a sweet-smiling always-there-for-you mom. A family with brothers and sisters who may have disagreements but, at the end of the day, value their relationship with their siblings, so they work to find a solution to problems.

But when you hear the actors of the Brady Bunch tell their behind the scenes stories, you find insecurities and backbiting, lustful affairs, and jealousies. So even in the land of make believe, the family struggles.

The family is God's creation. When the family works together in unity, it thrives. So the key is working together in unity. What does that look like and how do we obtain it?

The one who wars against our soul has been working to destroy the family unit since Genesis. In fact, Genesis is a great book to read to see family dysfunction up close and personal. I have learned a great deal from Genesis regarding people's tendencies, poor choices, and how God responds. God is incredibly forgiving; however, He does not excuse us from the ramifications of our choices, good or bad.

So how do we obtain a family of unity?

Start with truth; God's Word is Truth. Next, we must apply this truth in our lives. This will teach us the attributes to put on and the attributes and things that need to be put off. An example of this is pouring a clear liquid into a glass filled with a dark liquid. As the clear liquid goes in, the dark liquid is pushed out. And so it is with the Word of God. God's Word, which is alive and active, comes into our lives and pushes out the darkness. Now please keep in mind that this is a process not an overnight miracle!

So what does this have to do with family and unity? *Everything!*

When we decide to take in God's Word through study and learn to apply what we read to our lives, God's Word takes root, and we are putting on the attributes of Christ. God's Word takes our focus off of ourselves and our needs and places it on others. When we are others focused, we are now moving toward unity. Letting others go first and not pushing our way through creates unity.

We all come with some sort of baggage. We need the One who created the universe, who breathed life into us, who knit us together in our mothers' wombs, who taught us wisdom in that secret place, and who knows each one of us intimately to affirm His love for us. We all desire to belong and to be loved.

Back to my history, so you know a little bit about me. I grew up in a home where alcohol was prevalent, and so was alcoholism. My parents divorced when I was young, and soon I inherited a stepfather, who moved us to a city to be closer to his work. I was involved with Alateen, a program for the children of alcoholics.

Throughout my teen years, I felt unloved and unwanted. My mom, who had issues of her own, would kick me out of the house when we weren't getting along, which was often. Then she would call the police to find me and bring me home. I spent many nights on a friend's sofa or bedroom floor or sleeping in the woods.

A friend in the seventh grade tried to convince me to come live with her at a children's home. She said I would be happier there. But that didn't happen.

An older gentleman from our apartment building who worked with wayward kids said that he was going to send me to a camp for the summer. I was thrilled and looked forward to a change of scenery. But that didn't happen.

When I was fifteen years old, a girl from Alateen thought we should go live with her grandmother in Florida. So we hitchhiked to Florida. We were picked up by authorities and let go, picked up by an old man who gave us a ride, a meal, and then wanted to prostitute us. We left there, and we were eventually picked up again by the police. I was placed in a home for wayward kids, and she went on to her grandmother's house. I was to stay at that home until someone sent for me. Weeks went by, but no word came from anyone.

I was depressed, angry, unwanted, and unloved. I was wandering in the dark with no hope, no future, and no dreams.

One night, around midnight, I crept out of that home. I was so scared, ducking behind bushes every time I saw a light or car go by. Finally, I was free! Free? Hmmm…I hitchhiked back to Connecticut and got myself back into high school. A few days later, leaving school at the end of the day, while walking by a park, a large tree branch broke and fell on me, knocking me unconscious. I awoke in the hospital with tree bark in my hair, not knowing what had happened to me. I found out that a branch which spanned the width of the street fell on me. This left me very sore but with only bruises, or so I thought. I was released into my mother's care.

Several days later, although still sore, I went back to school. I was called to the office. My mother was there. She pointed at me and said, "I never want to see her again!"

I was whisked away to a nearby children's home and given a hospital bed in a wing that cared for wayward children. I lived there through my sixteenth birthday. The hospital worked diligently to find me a foster home, but nothing was available. One night, after midnight, I crept out of that hospital and hitchhiked to New Hampshire, where my dad lived. I stayed with him for several months, until one night when he came home drunk. I could see the loneliness in his eyes. Then he went to kiss me good night, and I realized this was not a good place for me.

I built large walls around my heart to protect it from any more pain or disappointment, and I learned to take care of myself and to count only on myself. But that is not where my story ends.

You see, "The God who sees me" (Genesis 16:13) was watching, drawing, loving, caring, and protecting. His loving kindness was pulling me in, for it is "His kindness that leads us to repentance" (Romans 2:4).

That branch that fell on me was the trauma that initiated a condition now called fibromyalgia, a waxing and waning of pain throughout the body. As the years passed, the pain increased, many times taking me to the brink of suicide. I could hear the enemy that wars against my soul whispering, "People will understand. The pain is too great, too much to bear. You can end the pain." Then the Savior would say, "Suicide? Is this the legacy you want to leave for your children? Are you saying there is no hope? Where there is Christ, there is hope. My grace is sufficient for you."

The God of all hope began to fill me with joy and peace as I trusted in Him, and I began to overflow with hope through the power of the Holy Spirit.

This woman who now writes to bring hope to others has been made new. I am alive in Christ! I am no longer defined by the words *depressed, angry, hurt, unwanted,* or *unloved.* I am now called chosen, wanted, beloved, child of the King.

God's grace and love saw me, called me and, upon my response to Him, began a work that He will see through to completion. I no longer wander in the darkness, for I have seen a great light. I am no longer independent but interdependent, "for we are all Living Stones fitted jointly together" (1 Peter 2:5). I have been healed from fibromyalgia. I have been healed from anger and depression through forgiveness. I am now defined by the words written on the pages of the Bible, and I hide them in my heart. I am now compelled to share the love and hope that is available to every single person who still has breath in him (or her).

"Because of His great love for us, God who is rich in mercy made us alive in Christ even when we were dead in transgressions" (Ephesians 2:4).

"How great is the love the Father has lavished_on us that we should be called children of God and that is what we are!" (1 John 3:1).

This is my story.

CHAPTER 2

❦

The Rocket

When my son, Marc, was eight, he received as a gift an Estes Rocket that he could launch high into the sky. It would deploy a parachute and float back down to the ground. Marc loved that rocket. (See photo.)

One afternoon, he was getting it ready to launch and called me outside to watch. It was a gorgeous day with a gentle breeze and warm sunshine. The look of excitement and anticipation was all over his face, and it was contagious! I found myself getting giddy with expectation just watching him. Marc lit the fuse, and that rocket shot straight up into the sky. Up, up, up, it went so far that we lost sight of it and were squinting our eyes and craning our necks toward the sky.

We waited patiently for the parachute to deploy, figuring that we would then catch sight of its location and what direction we would need to move to retrieve it.

We waited and waited and waited and searched throughout that blue sky, but as the minutes ticked by, excitement began to turn into disappointment. The disappointment was evident, for it caused Marc's shoulders to slouch down and his face to look forlorn.

Have you ever had a day like that? As a child of the King, you know full well that you are in the palm of His hand. You can pray, and heaven hears and moves. You can speak the Word of God boldly and feel the power of that Word. You awake in the morning with your heart and mind stayed on Him. You arise with anticipation, even excitement for what would unfold that day.

But by midmorning, the day takes an unexpected turn. You slowly feel the joy in your heart and smile on your face go south, and instead you experience anxiety, aggravation, disappointment, sadness, and frustration.

The expectation and wonder has been sidelined, and you are left looking for your lost keys, misplaced wallet, the one matching shoe, having to change a flat tire or wait for someone else to do it so you can get to your appointment. You've now moved into the role of referee for your children who are lunging at each other, fighting and bickering.

You are desperately trying to recall a single Bible verse to sway your mind and emotions back to that place of peace, joy, and rest. Then comes the accusatory voice in your head. You're not a very good Christian, you know. Look at how you are handling the situation, look how quickly you are coming unglued, unhinged even... There must not have been stability in the first place. I am sure that sister so and so would be able to keep it together and perhaps find a hymn to hum in the midst of these unforeseen circumstances.

Let me pause to say that we concede too quickly to that boney-fingered accuser. For the truth is that in this world, we *will* have trials and tribulations of many kinds—spouses, children, neighbors, bosses, and the like—but take heart for He, the Lover of your soul, has overcome the world. And you abide in Him.

So here I was, standing with my son, Marc, knowing full well that we were going to have to look for that rocket. So I said, "Marc, let's pray and ask God to show us where this rocket touched down. After all, He is the God of the universe. He made the stars and calls them by name. He spoke into existence all that we see and fashioned and formed Adam out of the dust. Certainly He can reveal where your rocket landed."

And so we prayed with anticipation that God certainly would show us, after all, we are His kids, and He loves us. Then we set out to comb the neighborhood to find the rocket.

Initially we were energetically looking in front yards and backyards, expecting God to answer our prayer and reveal this hidden rocket. As the minutes turned to hours, that sinking feeling began to rear its ugly head, saying, "Didn't God hear your prayer? Why is He taking so long to answer? Is this even important to Him? Does He care?"

Those voices seem to take every opportunity to seep into my conscience and lie about the awesomeness of my God and my right standing in Christ. That voice that suggests, "If you prayed more or spent more time in His presence, He would respond quicker."

But what does God's truth say?

"The Lord hears when I call to him" (Psalm 4:3).

"The righteous cry out, and the Lord hears them" (Psalm 34:17).

"Evening, morning and noon I cry out in distress, and He hears my voice" (Psalm 55:17).

"He fulfills the desires of those who fear him; He hears their cry and saves them" (Psalm 145:19).

"He hears the prayer of the righteous" (Proverbs 15:29).

Amen?

So at this point, Marc and I had split up and looked everywhere within the radius that we thought this rocket could have possibly gone but to no avail. The afternoon was almost over, and I had to head off to work at Pizza Pal. The sadness that overwhelmed me was palpable. The heaviness in my heart was unbearable. I told Marc that he only had a little more daylight, and that we could resume our search tomorrow morning.

I can still see him walking away from me with his shoulders slumped and his feet dragging, no longer expecting, no longer anticipating.

As I drove away from the house on my way to work, I burst out in tears and began proclaiming, "Nothing in all creation is hidden from God's sight. Everything is uncovered and laid bare before the eyes of Him to whom we must give account" (Hebrews 4:13).

You know all things, O God! Certainly You know where this rocket is. I had driven several blocks when a glimmer caught my eye, and I had an impulse to stop and look there. I reasoned there is no way that rocket came this far; it must have been the sun shining on that hubcap, so I kept driving. However, the impression to go back and look overwhelmed me. And so I turned my car around and headed back to see.

I stopped the car and got out to look at the place where I saw that glimmer with my peripheral vision. Under the car, behind the front tire, there it was—the rocket! How in the world did it get so far from where it was launched?

My entire body was now filled with thanksgiving and joy. I was shouting thanks to God, the God that sees, the God who hears, the God who knows all things! I just had to go back home and show my son. I could not wait to see the expression on his face. I was crying and singing and squealing with elation. My heart was leaping out of my chest with sheer joy. I was thanking God for His faithfulness to answer prayer, especially for Marc's sake. To build up his faith, knowing that when he prays, God certainly hears. To establish in his heart and mind this very day as a memorial of God's faithfulness, so in the future, he could remember, and this memory could bring hope.

Memorials are so very important because we humans tend to be shortsighted. So it is important that we diary in our heart, mind, and on paper the goodness of our God. So when we are faced with difficult circumstances, and that accusatory voice starts talking *smack* about our God, we can whip out our boney little finger and begin to cite all of the monumental times our God has moved on our behalf. Beginning with His Son, Jesus, taking our place on the cross, then raising Him to life for all of eternity. He has healed my disease, multiplied my resources, made me whole, gave me an enduring love for my husband, and so much more.

I was determined to show Marc the rocket, and so immediately, I drove back home. As I drove closer to my son, I could see the disappointment and discouragement all over his countenance and in his body language. I drove up and rolled down my window. Marc barely looked up.

I asked him, "Did you find it yet?"

He replied with a solemn, "No."

I asked him, "Did we pray and ask God to reveal where this rocket landed?"

He said, "Mom, you know we did."

I asked him, "Do you think God heard our prayer?"

Marc shrugged his shoulders.

I responded, "James says that 'the effectual, fervent prayer of a righteous man [and woman] availeth much.'" And if we needed evidence…here it is!" I held up the rocket.

Marc's eyes lit up, and his expression changed to sheer joy. He began to yell, "Yeah! Yeah!" pumping his fist in the air.

We hugged and thanked God for hearing our prayer and showing us the location of the rocket.

I went off to work proclaiming the goodness of God all the way there and throughout the evening. I could barely contain myself and shared this story with my coworkers and customers alike.

That day was a roller coaster of emotion. The enemy who wars against our souls took every opportunity to try to discourage, to speak lies, to encourage me to get my eyes *on* my surroundings and take my eyes *off* of my Heavenly Father and His Truth.

But our God remained the same. He did not change. He does not change. He is the same yesterday, today, and forever.

Our sensory perception can lie to us.

Our emotions can tell us that God doesn't hear, doesn't care, that we are on our own…we must not listen to our emotions.

Our circumstances, what we see with our eyes, can tell us that we should give up. We hear that there are not enough resources to meet our need. We do not listen to our circumstances.

Our mind can reason, and well-meaning voices in our lives may tell us that it no longer makes sense to hope for a different outcome.

But…we hope against all hope.

For we serve a God who is outside of our circumstances, who has unlimited resources, who is in the business of seeking and saving that which is lost. He *is* hope.

He has a history of multiplying a small lunch to feed thousands with leftovers. He has raised the dead and healed the sick. He made the lame to walk and the blind to see. He is a very present help in times of trouble. He is a Shield to those who take refuge in him.

He will never leave nor forsake. He will be with you always, even unto the ends of the earth.

He has always done what He said he would do and will continue to do so, for He is the God that sees…Amen? Amen!

CHAPTER 3

The Waxing and Waning Pain of Fibromyalgia

Y ou may be wondering, what about fibromyalgia? I was fifteen when I was walking home from school, and as I crossed the street, an oak tree branch broke away from the tree and fell on me. I have absolutely no recollection of hearing the cracking of the limb or seeing it fall toward me. I only have a friend who was an eyewitness account, the bark and tree debris in my hair and on my person at the hospital and the article from the newspaper with the heading, "Girl Gets Hit by Falling Tree Branch."

It is my understanding that fibromyalgia can begin with trauma. I believe this incident to be the trauma that opened the door to fibromyalgia in my life. The pain began a few years later in my lower torso. Once a month, during my period, the pain was most unbearable. Warm compresses and heating pads provided no relief.

I began going to a doctor to find relief. I had several minor surgeries when doctors determined that I had endometriosis, but I found no real relief for this incredible relentless pain in my torso.

Eventually, since I was not planning to have more children, my doctor recommended a hysterectomy. He reasoned that this should at least reduce the monthly pain. It took several months for me to recover from this surgery.

The one silver lining was that I lost weight and finally reached my dream weight. However, it turns out that my dream weight caused my face to look drawn. So what I thought was a dream weight only made me look very unhealthy. Lesson learned: Be the weight that your body is comfortable with and don't strive for some unreachable and unrealistic goal.

Over the years, the pain slowly made its way up my back between my shoulders and wrapped around my neck and head. It moved down my legs then into my knees. The pain was always present. The pressure in my neck caused migraines that were debilitating. There were times when it was relentless for weeks and would bring me to the brink of suicide. I would call my pastor's wife and sweet friend, Angela, to tell her that the pain was too much; I didn't think I could make it through the day. We would talk it out, pray, and the Lord would give me grace to make it through, telling me, "My grace is sufficient for you."

I finally sought help from a specialist to find out what was happening to me. He provided medicine to help ease the pain. I was also included in a study since others had the same types of pain, and doctors did not have a prognosis. For a month, I carried a device that would beep at different times of day, and I would be asked if I was experiencing pain in certain areas of my body, and if so, what was the level of pain. At the end of each day, I filled out a questionnaire describing my day, my level of pain, and how I coped. A nurse would visit me once a week and collect the data and check for "points of pain."

This study provided the information doctors needed to put a name to this disease, "fibromyalgia," which is defined by "points of pain." There are up to eighteen points of pain, and eleven points are required for a diagnosis.

As I stated, the doctor provided medicine to address the pain. However, my body seemed to adjust to new medicine within months. Over time, we ran out of the different types of available pain meds. I was told there was nothing more that medicine could do for me.

Having to endure constant pain can wear on you. Over time, it affects your desire to make plans because you don't know how you are going to feel at a future time. It causes you to pull away and isolate. I found it difficult to get out of bed most days, but my children were young, and they needed to get up, get dressed, eat, and get to school, and I still had to work full time.

My Heavenly Father taught me to make short goals. Just get up and get the kids breakfast, then if you don't feel well, you can go back to bed. Get dressed and go to work, then if you don't feel well, go home at lunch. Finish your workday, then you can go home and go to bed. Make dinner, then go to bed early. Short goals would get me through each day.

My Heavenly Father also taught me to get organized. Always put my car keys in the same place, and even on days when my mind could not process due to pain, I would out of habit go to the same place for my car keys. In the future, this organization would help me in a new career, which would require organization and attention to detail.

As I mentioned, the pain at times would hinder my ability to process information. So if you spoke to me, I could hear your words, but I was unable to put them together to make sense. I could not understand what you were saying to me.

I suffered for over twenty years with fibromyalgia. In hindsight, I see that God allowed this in my life to break down the walls that I had built around my heart and to show me that I could trust Him.

This might seem harsh to some, but I know, without a doubt, that the walls I had built around my heart were high and fortified. My attitude was one of independence: I can do it myself, and I don't need anybody. I needed God, my Heavenly Father to demonstrate His love toward me. He put me in a place where I had to depend on Him. He showed me through those years that He would never leave or forsake me. He comforted me and reminded me over and over that He cared for me and was more interested in making me whole than making me comfortable.

I can remember days when the pain would dissipate, and God would whisper, "I am in control. I have allowed this pain into your life. It is beneficial." Those pain-free days were like a gift, and I treasured them.

There were days when I could not get out of bed. My body was stiff from pain and completely exhausted from lack of sleep. Fibromyalgia impedes your ability to get deep (REM) sleep. So you wake up exhausted. If you don't sleep well, you experience more pain. When you experience more pain, you don't sleep well. It is a vicious cycle.

Chronic pain can wear on you. It can cause you to isolate since you don't "feel up to" going out or being with people. It makes it difficult to plan future events since you don't know how you will feel on that day, so you don't make plans. Not making plans over time isolates, you from the people that care about you. Isolation allows the one who wars against your soul to speak lies. "If God loves you, why does He let you suffer?" Isolation leads to depression.

Depression over time creates hopelessness. That hopelessness can take you down roads that you never thought you would travel.

If you are suffering, please get in touch and stay in touch with people. We are designed to be interdependent, not independent. Please see isolation as a red flag and call someone.

May God's grace and peace rest on you.

CHAPTER 4

When You Are about Your Father's Business, Your Needs Will Be Met

I t was Christmas Eve. I had just gotten out of work and still had several items on my gift list. I went to Caldor's to shop. Caldor's was similar to Walmart. As I entered the store, I saw people scurrying about, grabbing toys from the shelves. Two people were playing tug-of-war with a scarf since it was the last one. The store was a madhouse with boxes and cartons strewn about, and people were mindlessly grabbing anything they could get their hands on. The mood was characterized by stress and anger rather than the wonder of Christmas. People were arguing over stuff!

I looked around to see if I could find the few things on my list. As I wandered through the store, I became increasingly sad. Lord, this must really hurt your heart. The Magi presented Jesus with gifts of gold, frankincense, and myrrh, and so we give gifts. But the scene in this store was far from the Magi who came to worship Jesus.

All of the checkout lines were extremely long, so I selected one and stepped in line. The clerks looked tired, and the people in line were impatient and complaining. I looked around at all the people and began to pray. First for the clerks and their families, then for each person standing in line. The Lord gave me insight and glimpses of the needs of these people. I silently prayed asking God to once more show them the true meaning of Christmas. A baby sent from heaven, who would be entrusted to a young girl and her betrothed. But that baby would show the world God's Word in the flesh, for Jesus was the Word made flesh. That baby would grow in stature and favor with God and man. He would live a sinless life and then become the spotless lamb. He would be the atoning sacrifice that would bridge the gap to the Father. For no man comes to the Father except through Jesus. He would suffer, die, and be buried in a borrowed tomb. His disciples would feel hopeless and helpless until the third day. On the third day, He would rise and take His place at the right hand of the Father. Christmas is about the Lion of Judah, who came as a spotless lamb.

I began praying for everyone within my sight. I asked the Lord for wisdom to help me pray. I envisioned each person and prayed regarding the struggles that they may be experiencing. I prayed for their salvation. As I prayed, my line began moving forward. My line was very long, but it appeared that I was moving forward at a quicker pace than the rest of the lines until I was face-to-face with the clerk. I thanked her for working on Christmas Eve.

As I reached for my packages, the Lord impressed on me, "When you are about my Father's business, I will always take care of you."

I have never forgotten that principal.

Lord, each day, may I be aware of the people and the need around me to initiate prayer for these individuals as you prompt me. May I never be too focused and busy with my own life that I forget there are so many others who could benefit from a kind word, a gentle glance, or a caring smile. Keep me sensitive to the needs around me. Lord, let me be like Peter who's very shadow healed. May I always take the time to feed your sheep and care for your lambs. Amen.

Chapter 5

Have You Considered My Servant?

Anyone who has ever lived in close proximity with their neighbors can identify with this chapter. For six years, we lived on the first floor of a two-family house. We had some great neighbors move into the second floor. We also had some not-so-great neighbors.

A single mom and her two children would be placed in the not-so-great category. As they were moving into the second floor, I was praying for them and hoping to be able to minister whenever needed.

After a few months, my husband shared with me that when I would go off to work, on numerous occasions, the woman upstairs would come down and ask to borrow a tool, ask for help hanging a picture, or sometimes want to share her baked goods. He questioned if I thought this woman was making advances. I retorted, "Are you putting out a vibe that says you are available? If not, then kindly let her know that you are married and not interested in any extracurricular activities."

I have heard it said that there is nothing worse than a woman scorned. I am not sure I believe that statement; however, I can attest that living with a woman scorned is not a walk in the park.

Over the next several months, this woman put on her high heels as soon as she stepped out of bed and wore them all day walking throughout the house. From the moment she awoke in the morning until she went to bed, she was heavy stepping all through the house.

Her children took pleasure in dumping things like flour or water out the second-floor window onto my daughter's head when she was outside and within striking distance.

Needless to say, I was praying for a solution to this dilemma. Through the months that passed, I did not always keep my emotions intact and, unfortunately from time to time, allowed them to fuel my conversation, which I deeply regret.

This family eventually moved out, and I was relieved to have a reprieve.

Let me note here that it has been my experience that the Lord in His grace provides opportunity to make amends. If I have not conducted myself as I should, the Lord will cause me and this person to cross paths again. This woman showed up one Christmas at a rest home where our choir was singing. Since I was narrating, I had opportunity to be front and center and look her in the eye throughout the program. At the end of the program, I quickly made my way toward her and asked if she would please forgive me for my past behavior. She nodded, and I wished her a very Merry Christmas and God's best for her and her family.

Thank you, Lord, for your goodness and immense wisdom in allowing me to make amends so that my past behavior is not a stumbling block for someone to know you, and that I can learn from those past mistakes and not have to live in those regrets.

I began to pray regarding the next tenant, and I asked God to send someone who loved Him, and with whom, I could fellowship. After all, I was raising two children, working full time, and I was young in my walk with the Lord. I needed a little solace in my home.

A few months went by, then one day, the new tenant arrived and began moving into the second floor. Only a few weeks went by, and I came home to find my back door had been broken into, and my basement filled with this new tenant's items. I made my way up the back staircase where this woman met me. I explained that the basement was not included in her rental, and she would need to remove her things. This large woman grabbed me, put me in a choke hold. As she squeezed tight, she said, "Do you know how easy it would be to snap your skinny little neck? Don't mess with me."

She then pushed me down the stairs. As I lay on the landing, trying to recover from this unexpected assault, I saw out the back door a neighbor in their backyard and thought of yelling for help. But I was not really hurt, just shaken up, so I opted to slowly, quietly get up and go back into my kitchen.

Maybe thirty minutes went by, and the doorbell rang. It was the police, who were responding to a report from this tenant that she had been assaulted by me! I contacted the landlord who would not confirm to the police that the square footage of the basement was strictly part of my rental agreement.

The landlord did inform me that this woman is considering a rent-to-own agreement for this house. Well, that explains why he was willing to turn a blind eye to this woman overtaking my rental space.

Over the next several weeks, this tenant proceeded to overtake the rest of our basement recreation room with her stuff. If annoyed, she would call the police and place false reports. Once she reported that my husband threatened her with a gun, which caused numerous police to surround our home. Thankfully his hunting rifles were not confiscated, and no charges were placed against him.

The next few months were a chain of events that left me exhausted and angry at God for allowing this woman to move into this house.

Jennifer, Marc, and I were at an evening service, and I do not recall what was being preached from the pulpit, but I could not sit and listen one more minute. I signaled to my children that we were leaving, and I walked out in the middle of that service.

I was angry at God for allowing this woman to move here! So angry that I wanted to turn my back and walk away. Angela called me and shared that times are hard right now, but it is so important that you move toward God and not away from Him. It felt as though I was in limbo while hanging on to this anger. I could not move. I was stuck in this place of incredible hurt and pain and truly not wanting to release it.

You may have found yourself in a place like this at some point in your life. Our natural human instinct when we are hurt is to back away, to not want anything to do with the person who has hurt us. We plan in our mind how we can avoid this person moving forward.

We as humans automatically desire to withdraw after a conflict. We want to remain in our anger because it is comfortable. It is what we know. I had a decision to make. Who or what would I turn to at this time of crisis in my life?

In my anger, I wanted to turn away from God, but where would I go? The only reason I have life is because God gave it to me. He redeemed me and put a new song in my heart. His Word defines who I am. If I walk away, where could I go? What then defines me? Who then would I be?

I cried out, "You have the power to do all things, God! I asked for a reprieve, and you sent this woman. Why, God, why would you send this woman?"

"I sent her to you so that you would love her," God responded.

"What?"

"I sent her to you so that you would love her," God repeated.

This response completely changed my composure from a stiff angry woman to almost a puddle on the floor. This response completely took me off guard. The fact that God would entrust to me this soul. That He would send her to *me* to fulfill His plan.

Back in the day, before digital photos, grandmothers would carry in their wallet a plastic accordion-folded photo insert that held wallet-sized photos of their kids and grandkids called a Brag Book. At any time, grandma could proudly pull out this plastic insert, and it would systematically unfold all the way to the ground to show off all her loved ones.

That is the visual that God gave me. He impressed on me that just as that grandma takes pleasure in showing off her loved ones, God also takes pleasure in His loved ones.

"Then the Lord said to Satan, 'Have you considered my servant Job? There is no one on earth like him; he is blameless and upright, a man who fears God and shuns evil'" (Job 1:8).

God was bragging to Satan about Job.

In like manner, God still says to Satan today, "Have you considered my servant, _____? You place your name in the blank." God brags about His kids. He too has a brag book! I am in it! So are you if you have accepted His son, Jesus, and are being transformed by His Word.

You may think that you certainly could *not* be compared to Job! Why not? Job was a man who feared God and shunned evil. Do you fear God and shun evil?

Job was blameless and upright. "Well," you may say, "I am certainly not blameless."

Based on 1 John 1:9, *if we confess our sins, he is faithful and just to forgive us our sins and cleanse us from all unrighteousness.*

So we become blameless and upright when we confess our sins because of God's forgiveness and cleansing.

So what does the Word say about the upright?

"Solomon answered, 'You have shown great kindness to your servant, my father David, because he was faithful to you and righteous and upright in heart'" (1 Kings 3:6).

"For the Lord is righteous, he loves justice; the upright will see his face'" (Psalm 11:7).

"Rejoice in the Lord and be glad, you righteous; sing, all you who are upright in heart!" (Psalm 32:11).

"May integrity and uprightness protect me, because my hope, Lord, is in you" (Psalm 25:21).

"Sing joyfully to the Lord, you righteous; it is fitting for the upright to praise him" (Psalm 33:1).

"My shield is God Most High, who saves the upright in heart'" (Psalm 7:10).

So we see that God saves the upright in heart, a heart that loves what God loves and hates what God hates. A heart that desires to do His will over I will. A heart that fears God and shuns evil.

It is important that we remember the characters in the Bible were real people who really lived. The Bible is filled with human examples; some served God. Some served themselves or other gods. But they were all real people with human emotion.

Job 1 continues, "'Does Job fear God for nothing?' Satan replied. 'Have you not put a hedge around him and his household and everything he has? You have blessed the work of his hands so that his flocks and herds are spread throughout the land.'"

Did you get that snapshot?

Because Job was blameless and upright, feared God and shunned evil, a hedge of protection was placed around him and his household and everything he had. The work of his hands was blessed!

"For the eyes of the Lord range throughout the earth to strengthen those whose hearts are fully committed to him" (2 Chronicles 16:9).

So then why did God allow that woman to move into that apartment and mess with you and your family? You may be wondering. Because I was in God's brag book! He could trust me to show love to this woman if He asked me. To be sure, He was also fully protecting me, even though this woman's choices affected my life and my comfort. As I previously stated, the fact that God would send someone to me with the purpose of showing them His love completely melted me.

I sat down with my children, Jennifer and Marco, and explained that we are going to kneel at this sofa daily and pray for this woman. We are going to show her the love of God. We are going to ask God to soften her heart. We are going to pray Ezekiel 36:26: "I will give you a new heart and put a new spirit in you; I will remove from you your heart of stone and give you a heart of flesh." That is what we did.

Please note that showing the love of God does not make you a welcome mat. On the contrary, God's love sets boundaries. God's love is strong and fights for a person, always hoping that they will turn to Him and, in doing so, be changed forever by His love and forgiveness. So then, they may go and do likewise for others.

So after that, we all lived happily ever after—NOT!

Sometimes when you begin to pray for a person, it turns up the heat! Things did not get better right away.

One day, I walked out of my front door and confronted this woman who had just pulled into the driveway with another person in the passenger seat of her car. I looked this woman in the eye and said, "I am not afraid of you, though you would like me to be. You are not here by chance. God brought you to this place and into my life. My children and I are praying for you to experience the love of God and His forgiveness. Perfect love casts out all fear."

I confidently but not arrogantly walked back into my house.

Several weeks passed, and the police contacted me. The neighbors reported someone breaking into my bedroom window. The police had investigated and discovered a school girl had indeed climbed through my bedroom window and helped herself to a soda from the fridge before heading upstairs to her mother's apartment.

Yes. This woman's daughter had taken her mother's lead and followed suit by modeling the same behavior of breaking in and taking whatever she wanted.

But my neighbor's (hedge of protection) were looking out for me and reported what they saw. I came home as the authorities were arresting the young girl and questioning her mother.

Upon seeing me, Carol broke into tears and apologized to me for her daughter's behavior. (Not hers, but that was a start, right?) She shared how her daughter has been a real handful and has had to be removed from her home at times and placed in a center for wayward children. As a parent, my heart broke for her. No one wants to experience the pain of a prodigal child.

I asked if I may pray for her and her daughter. She nodded through the tears, and I bowed my head. I thanked God for the privilege to pray for this woman and her daughter and told God that I forgive them for the wrongs committed against me and my family. I prayed that they would move toward him to find hope, peace, and rest.

That was an incredible day! Thank you, Lord, for the book of Job. How incredibly *huge* Your brag book must be! I am so very grateful to be in it!

CHAPTER 6

Suicide: Is This the Legacy that You Want to Leave?

As I have previously stated, the unrelenting pain from fibromyalgia on several occasions had me contemplating suicide. I would envision driving my car off a cliff at a high rate of speed that would most certainly kill me. But the Lord would whisper, "Is this the legacy that you want to leave? Are you saying there is no hope? Then you are saying there is no Christ, for where there is Christ there is hope." God's truth would again stabilize me and remind me that He will never leave me nor forsake me. He is with me, and therefore, I have hope. He will walk me through, not necessarily keep me from the pain.

For several days, the pain that wrapped around my head was overwhelming to the point that now it was more than I could bear.

One of the methods to relieve pain that I was taught was to wrap myself tightly in a blanket, and the heat from my body would begin to soothe the pain. One evening, I was wrapped tightly in a blanket, lying in the dark, asking God to please either free me from this pain or take me home.

As I lay in bed in that dark room, I was reminded of the handgun in the top drawer of my husband's dresser. "People will understand. They have watched you suffer from this disease for quite some time. They will be glad that you are now pain free." The words *pain free* began to resonate in my mind and became so appealing. I was entranced with the notion that I could end this pain today. "People will understand. The pain is too much to bear." I went deeper into this lethargic state. Again the thought of the handgun in the top drawer. "It's too much to bear." I began to visualize getting up and walking toward the dresser, opening the drawer, embracing the gun, and laying back down.

The thought of being pain free was so alluring.

I was captivated by the notion that I could be free from pain. I fell deeper and deeper into this trancelike state. The words *pain free* resonating in my mind. I was almost giddy with the thought that tonight could end it all. I became convinced in my mind that this was the right thing to do. Again I saw myself getting up and walking toward the dresser, opening the drawer, embracing the gun, and laying back down.

As I visualized again the gun in the drawer and prepared to get up and retrieve it, there was a knock at the back door. It startled me and brought me back to my senses. How in the world could I think such a thing? My children are in the house. Again a knock at the back door. I got up and answered the door. It was the girl upstairs asking if Jennifer was home.

I am so grateful that God sent that young lady to knock on my door and shake me out of that state. I can certainly understand how a person can get caught in that downward spiral. The notion that whatever pain one has been enduring, whether physical or mental could end, is very seductive. How the one who wars against our souls can whisper promises of freedom!

However, this is not the legacy that I want to leave. The enemy would have loved for me to have taken my life because then he could boast. You see, Colossians 2:15 tells me, "And having disarmed the powers and authorities, he made a public spectacle of them, triumphing over them by the cross." So anytime the enemy that wars against our souls can make a public spectacle of us and show that he has not been disarmed, and the cross is a sham, he boasts.

But my hope is found in nothing less than Jesus's blood and His righteousness. That is the legacy that I want to leave. For where there is Christ, there is hope!

If you find yourself in a place where the enemy that wars against your soul is taunting you with gaining freedom of pain by taking your life, tell someone, disarm him, talk about it, do not let it remain a secret, where he can draw you in to that place by his seductive words. Tell someone! Get help!

Remember, "now the Lord is the Spirit, and where the Spirit of the Lord is, there is freedom" (2 Corinthians 3:17).

I do not know what type of pain you may be experiencing. Whether your pain is physical, or mental, or both. But I do know the Great Physician. I do know that God's Word does not change. The Lord can give you a new perspective, His perspective, which is a much bigger picture. He can walk you through this time in your life if you let Him. Please let Him.

CHAPTER 7

Seasons of Our life

One beautiful New England fall Sunday, I was driving to church and admiring the leaves changing colors. The beauty of the reds, yellows, and greens of the leaves was spectacular.

Wow, God, your creation is amazing! The leaves are so beautiful!

"The leaves have to die in order for their colors to come forth," the Lord whispered. This impressed on me that when *we* die to self, God's beauty can come forth in *our* lives.

Now I understand that scientifically the following happens: chlorophyll breaks down. In the fall, because of changes in the length of daylight and changes in temperature, the leaves stop their food-making process. The chlorophyll breaks down; the green color disappears; and the yellow, orange, and red colors become visible and give the leaves part of their fall splendor.

Note the following: As the fall colors appear, other changes are taking place. At the point where the stem of the leaf is attached to the tree, a special layer of cells develops and gradually severs the tissues that support the leaf. At the same time, the tree seals the cut so that when the leaf is finally blown off by the wind or falls from its own weight, it leaves behind a leaf scar.

We too go through seasons, a mountaintop season, a valley season. Seasons when we can hear the voice of God so clearly and seasons when He seems distant, and we feel dry. Seasons with incredible pain and seasons with exuberant joy!

If you don't like the season you are currently in, then take heart in knowing that seasons of our lives change much like the seasons in New England. Know that there is a bigger picture, and that other changes are taking place that allows for your colors to come forth.

God, your creation is incredible! Help me to continue to die to self so that my very best colors may come forth.

CHAPTER 8

God, Give Me Love for this Man

I have been married for thirty-eight years. I have learned that marriages go through changes, seasons if you will. Initially everything is new. You are newlyweds, and the novelty of marriage brings with it a fresh vibrancy. Children may be born, and with each newborn comes new challenges.

Over time, as each of you take care of your responsibilities, your relationship can become robotic. You both get up, have coffee, perhaps go off to work or stay home with the children, and then meet back at the dinner table to discuss that day's events. Eventually there may be no discussion just eating. Perhaps over time, dinner becomes a thing of the past, and you find yourselves living different lives.

Life is messy, and it can affect your relationship with your spouse. I know over time that is what happened with me. The Lord showed me a few things that I would like to share.

I was watching a movie one night, and the male character of the movie brushed the cheek of the female and then said something sweet. Immediately, the Lord shared, "Is that what you are expecting from your husband? Do you expect him to be like this fictional character? Do not forget that movies are not real life. They are made up of clever lines and scripts, which bring this character to life."

Could I be setting my husband up for failure by expecting him to be like this movie character? I think women especially can fall into this trap. The movie or book doesn't have to be a Harlequin romance novel. It could be a *Sleepless in Seattle* type of character or Andrew Paxton from *The Proposal.*

To this day, I am careful not to think, "I wish my husband was more like…"

I also had a season when I felt I could not love this man. We had experienced challenges with our children and many other issues, and I cried out to God, "I have no love for this man." I always felt so angry around him and could barely stand the thought of getting in bed with him. I was not in a good place. I told God, "You have to give me love for this man." God began to share with me what His love looked like. Not the romantic, butterflies-in-my-stomach kind of love but the long-term, committed, covenant love that He outlined in this word:

"Love is patient, love is kind. It does not envy, it does not boast, it is not proud. It does not dishonor others, it is not self-seeking, it is not easily angered, it keeps no record of wrongs. Love does not delight in evil but rejoices with the truth. It always protects, always trusts, always hopes, always perseveres. [God's] Love never fails," (1 Corinthians 13:4–8).

Okay, God. This is a tall order. The Lord shared, "It needs to begin with My presence in your life. When you abide in Me, you will remember how I loved you when you were so unlovable. How I pursued you and was patient with you. How My kindness led you to repentance. I no longer brought up your past as a weapon, but desired to heal those areas in your life. How I was long suffering, and I protected you. You learned where there is Christ there is hope."

I am always amazed that whenever I ask the Lord to change someone or a circumstance, He starts with changing my perspective! He gives me His perspective, then as I apply His Word, change happens. Usually in *me* first, and then my change affects others.

God showed me how to love this man, my husband. He showed me those areas that I needed to work on, and I listened and applied, not always successfully, but I am so very grateful to have a healthy and loving relationship with my husband today. But it did not come easy, and it did take work, anything worthwhile usually does.

CHAPTER 9

Worship: It's Not about You

I have been attending church services since the eighties. I found that if I had a week where I was faithful in daily prayer, paid close attention to my thought life, read my Bible, and was victorious through the battles of the week, it affected my worship on Sunday morning. I felt as though I had a right to come into His presence and worship Him. I found myself to be more boisterous and free to praise Him.

On the contrary, if I had a tough week or when I allowed my emotions to rule instead of the truth of God's Word, or I gave into the temptation that taunted me, or the secret sin, I found it hard to come into God's presence and praise Him. Many times, I found myself crying because I knew I should have represented Him better through the week. I felt very unworthy and found myself to be less enthusiastic and more introverted because of my lack of victory throughout that week.

For so many years, how I represented "the kingdom" throughout the week would affect my worship on Sunday.

Then one Sunday morning, the Lord impressed on me, "Sunday morning is not about you. Sunday morning and worship is about me, the great I am. Come into My presence and worship Me for who I am. Regardless of what happened throughout your week, it does not change who I am because I change not."

Come into my presence and declare who I am.

"I am the Way, The Truth and The Life" (John 14:6).

"I am the Good Shepherd" (John 10:11).

"I am the Bright and Morning Star" (Revelation 22:16).

"I am the Alpha and Omega" (Revelation 1:8, 21:6, 22:13).

"I am the Creator of the Universe" (Isaiah 43:15, Romans 1:25).

"I am your Rock" (Deuteronomy 32:4).

"I am your Provider" (Genesis 22:8).

"I am your Peace" (Isaiah 26:3).

"I am your Joy" (Nehemiah 8:10).

"I am the One who determines the number of the stars and call them each by name" (Psalm 147:4).

"I am your Shield, your very great reward" (Genesis 15:1).

"I am God Almighty" (Genesis 17:, 35:11).

"I am who I Am" (Exodus 3:4).

"I am the Lord, who heals you" (Exodus 15:26).

"I am the Lord your God, who brought you out of Egypt, out of bondage" (Leviticus 26:13, Numbers 15:41, Deuteronomy 5:6, Psalm 81:10).

Worship me for who I am, regardless of your week, I am worthy of all praise, so praise me for who I am. 'Cause, Nance...It's not about *you*. I am always worthy of praise. I am the God who changest not, and "Jesus Christ is the same yesterday and today and forever" (Hebrews 13:8). So worship me for who I am.

When life is hard, which can be often, because of the broken world that we live in, we bring the *sacrifice* of praise into the house of our God. We *choose* to praise God for who He is in the midst of our circumstances.

That praise is professing the names of God, the names of Jesus, and declaring who He is.

"Through Jesus, therefore, let us continually offer to God a sacrifice of praise—the fruit of lips that openly profess his name" (Hebrews 13:15).

Openly professing His name causes our spirit man to wake up, to strengthen, to stretch, since indeed this is the Word of God and His Word is alive and active. It comes alive within us and affects us when we speak it. The Word is the Logos of God, and it is powerful.

It is also imperative that we are thankful.

1 Thessalonians 5:16–18 states, "Rejoice always, pray continually, give thanks in all circumstances; for this is God's will for you in Christ Jesus." What does this look like? Is it putting on a mask and denying the hard circumstances of life, or the blow back we feel from other people's sin affecting us? Not at all.

We can rejoice always and be thankful because of who He is! We know we have a God in heaven who hears us when we pray, who knows the very darkest part of our thoughts and hearts, yet still sent His Son to die for us. We can "enter his gates with thanksgiving and his courts with praise; give thanks to him and praise his name" (Psalm 100:4) because of who He is and who He is in our lives! He is for us! We have become sons and daughters of God if we have accepted His Son and walk in His ways. Who He is in us brings hope to us and our circumstances since nothing is impossible for our God. He is limitless, the mountain mover and sustainer of life. He has a plan and a purpose for our lives, and He is able to recalculate when we take a wrong turn.

If I thought this life was it, and then we die, I am certain I would have cut my life short. But the reality is that the King of kings knows my name and cares deeply for me. He calls me friend and is the Lover of my soul. For this, I am thankful, and because of who He is, I will bring the sacrifice of praise and not just on a Sunday, but every moment I have breath.

I am so very grateful that…it's not about me. It's all about who He is!

He is Great and greatly to be praised!

CHAPTER 10

Guess Who Came to Dinner

My son, Marc, began to veer off the chosen path when he was a teenager. I could list reasons why, but the long and short of it is that he began making decisions that took him away from God's plans for his life. He chose to do his will over God's will. As a parent, when you see your child heading down that wayward road, it is heart-wrenching. I warned Marc that the road he was on would lead to jail or death. Those were the only two possible outcomes.

I remember the phone call so clearly. I was working at a pizza restaurant, and my daughter and her friend, Chris, were sitting in a booth, eating. It was a busy Thursday night at the pizza house, and the phone was ringing off the wall. In those days, the phone was actually connected to the wall.

I picked up and said my usual, "Pizza Pal, may I help you?" There was a slight pause on the other end, then came my son's voice, "Mom. I am so sorry, Mom."

My heart dropped, and I began to prepare myself for what would come next.

"Mom, I am so sorry. They said we were trespassing. I didn't know…"

I began half listening to the story that my son was weaving, waiting to hear the result and where he was. New Britain lockup. Well, he was warned that the path that he was on would lead only to death or jail. Thank you, Lord, for the latter. He has opportunity to repent.

My daughter could read my face from the booth; she knew something was wrong. I could see that she too was bracing herself for the news. Marc has been arrested; I told her and her friend, Chris. I don't have the facts, but I know he is currently in a jail cell.

After the dinner rush was over we took a ride to the police station and spoke with an officer, who provided a much different account. Marc and his friend had stolen a car and were caught and arrested. The officer told me that since this was Easter weekend, we would need to bail Marc out Thursday morning, or he would spend the holiday weekend in lockup. My response: Put the fear of God back into that boy. I will not be bailing him out. He had fair warning and chose this road, so he will have to cry out to his God for deliverance. I am not Marc's deliverer.

Jennifer, Chris, and I drove back to the pizza restaurant since I still had several hours to go before the restaurant closed. As we pulled into the parking lot, my husband drove up asked me what happened. I shared with him what the officer told me and my response. He did not agree with my perspective. He wanted Marc bailed out stating, "What kind of mother lets her son sit in jail?"

Marc was allowed to make several calls during his time in lockup.

His initial call was filled with half-truths and self-justification. I told Marc that he needed to repent. He should confess everything to God, starting with even a quarter that he may have stolen and ending with this stolen car. For 1 John 1:9 states, "If we confess our sins, he is faithful and just and will forgive us our sins and purify us from all unrighteousness." At that point, you may cry out for deliverance and see if God makes a way; however, you were warned, and there are consequences for our actions, good and bad.

Marc's stay in jail tore my husband apart. I have rarely seen my husband cry. He cried throughout that weekend. I knew we were in the midst of spiritual warfare. The enemy that wars against our souls wanted my son, and I was praying, "God, whatever it takes for Marc to serve you wholeheartedly, I am willing to endure. Have your way, he is yours Lord. Do as you see fit."

May I say that handing my son over to our Heavenly Father seems natural, but we as humans want to step in to obtain our desired outcome. We are notorious for manipulating the situation or just taking the ball and running with it, asking God to bless our plans. However, much prayer had been lifted to the heavens for Marc, and he made the choice that lead him to this place. If prison was required for change, then so be it. He is yours, Lord!

Marc was allowed phone calls in the morning and evening during his lockup, and with every new call came a little more brokenness. The phone call that I received from Marc on Sunday morning before I left for Easter service was what I wanted to hear. No excuses, no justification, no deflecting responsibilities to others. Marc said he was preparing for the judge to send him to the Hartford Corrections and knew that he deserved it.

I went to Easter service that morning and praised the Lord. First, because the Lord is worthy of all praise, and second, because my son had repented and is now in good standing with his Heavenly Father. When we are in right standing with our Heavenly Father, this positions us for God to work in our situations. We are ripe for a miracle.

After service, my husband, Jennifer, and I went to Easter dinner at his brother's house. That is where the most amazing event happened.

All the family was already there when we arrived, except my sister-in-law, Christine. We all chatted, but no one asked me about Marc, so I figured that everyone already knew his whereabouts.

The room was full of conversation, everyone catching up with each other's lives, when Christine arrived. She looked around the room and immediately asked, "Where's Marc?" Instantaneous silence. All eyes turned to me awaiting a response.

I replied, "He's been detained."

Christine pressed, "Detained like he'll be here later?"

"No," I responded. "Detained like he is in New Britain lockup and will not be arraigned until Monday morning."

"What happened?" she questioned.

So I explained the timeline of events leading up to this moment ending with, "I really don't know what I am going to do. I don't want to see him go to Hartford Corrections, but I am not his deliverer, and he was warned that if he continued down this path that this was a very possible outcome."

Just then, the young man sitting next to me, whom my beautiful niece, Alex, brought to dinner, turned to me and said, "Don't do anything. I'll take care of everything." He extended his hand to introduce himself, "Steve Angelillo, I am a bondsman for New Britain Superior Court. I'll take care of everything. You just go to work like it's a regular day." He continued, "People tend to pronounce my name Ang-e-lillo, but my grandfather is adamant that it is pronounced 'Angel-illo. Most people say Ang, but it is most definitely Angel."

To say that I was flabbergasted would be an understatement. The inside of my tummy got all giddy as I silently thanked God for entering into the situation. It is funny how we pray and anticipate God answering prayer, but when He does, it most often surprises us. Still to this day, I am surprised each time God answers prayer, and yet I pray expecting Him to answer. Silly humans!

As it turned out, everyone but Christine knew Marc's whereabouts because he had called them first asking for bail money. I am very glad that they declined because that left room for God to move.

Shortly after dinner, the phone rang. It was Marc. I could hear the brokenness in his voice. He told me he was ready to face the consequences of his actions, and he deserved those consequences. He had made peace with God and was ready for whatever sentence the judge handed down. He was broken and accepting responsibility for his actions.

"A broken and contrite heart, I will in no wise cast out," God whispered to me.

I passed the phone around the room and gave everyone opportunity to speak with Marc, and then I got back on the phone and said, "You'll never guess who came to dinner. Steve Angel-illo," I shared with Marc how Steve's grandfather was adamant that his name should be pronounced Angel not Ang.

So that was the answer from heaven. Marc was to be bonded out and put on a rehabilitation program for first offenders. He was not sent to Hartford Corrections. I wish the same could be said for his friend and partner in crime, who I understand had "priors." That young man eventually gave his life to Jesus and is currently walking in God's way—another answer to prayer. He has much "baggage" from the past that God continues to unpack and heal. Pray for Jaye because we all come to the cross with baggage from the past. Ideas, traditions, hurts, fears can all give us an idea of what God is like, but only Jesus, the Word made flesh who dwelt among us, gives us a clear picture.

I would like to say that Marc learned his lesson and stayed far away from the road that brought him to that jail cell, but old habits die hard, and we have to continually transform our minds with God's Word, for those cycles in our lives to be broken. It is not easy, and life gets messy. But there is hope in Christ.

Christ changes everything. We have a tendency to be short-sighted and just deal with this lifetime, but there is an afterlife for everyone who needs to be considered, and Christ makes all the difference in this life and the next.

Unfortunately, this one time in jail was the not the only time; however, patterns in someone's life are strongholds. Those strongholds sadly don't always come down quickly or easily, some by prayer and fasting.

Keep praying because as Marco would say, "The story switches."

CHAPTER 11

The Power of Speaking God's Word, Psalm 51

One day, I was heading home from working a relocation in Hartford and stopped to get some gas. As I searched through my wallet for my debit card, I noticed an older man carrying a plastic bag filled with what looked like pantry items. He was asking people for money. His posture was hunched over, and he made little to no eye contact with the people he was approaching. People coming in and out of the gas station and those pumping gas avoided making eye contact with him, perhaps in hopes that he would not approach them.

He asked me if I had a few dollars so that he could get something to eat. I looked into his plastic bag and saw a box of mac and cheese and a few other food items. I commented, "You have food items in your bag."

He responded, "I don't have anywhere to cook these things, and I'd really like a cheeseburger."

I was compelled to give him some cash, but knew I probably only had a dollar or two in my wallet. I reached for my wallet and was surprised to see a ten-dollar bill. I said, "I have ten dollars for you, please keep the food in your bag, but you have to promise that you will find a Bible and begin to read each day."

He replied, "I know Psalm 51!"

A little surprised, I inquired, "You know Psalm 51?"
He replied proudly, "Yea, I know Psalm 51."
I responded, "Nice! Let's hear it!"
He said, "Right here?"
I said, "Yes, right here, out loud."
He began...

> Have mercy on me, O God, according to your unfailing love; according to your great compassion blot out my transgressions. Wash away all my iniquity and cleanse me from my sin. For I know my transgressions, and my sin is always before me. Against you, you only, have I sinned and done what is evil in your sight; so you are right in your verdict and justified when you judge. Surely I was sinful at birth, sinful from the time my mother conceived me. Yet you desired faithfulness even in the womb; you taught me wisdom in that secret place. Cleanse me with hyssop, and I will be clean; wash me, and I will be whiter than snow. Let me hear joy and gladness; let the bones you have crushed rejoice. Hide your face from my sins and blot out all my iniquity. Create in me a pure heart, O God, and renew a steadfast spirit within me. Do not cast me from your presence or take your Holy Spirit from me. Restore to me the joy of your salvation and grant me a willing spirit, to sustain me.

As that hunched over, forlorn, lost, broken man spoke God's Word, the most amazing transformation took place. His stature began to straighten, and joy washed over his countenance.
He continued...

> Then I will teach transgressors your ways, so that sinners will turn back to you. Deliver me

from the guilt of bloodshed, O God, you who are God my Savior, and my tongue will sing of your righteousness. Open my lips, Lord, and my mouth will declare your praise. You do not delight in sacrifice, or I would bring it; you do not take pleasure in burnt offerings. My sacrifice, O God, is a broken spirit; a broken and contrite heart you, God, will not despise.

At this point, that man began to skip and leap in the air like a child outside at recess. He said to me, "I'm gonna see you in heaven!"

I could faintly hear the remainder of the Psalm as he crossed the street and moved on to get a cheeseburger.

May it please you to prosper Zion, to build up the walls of Jerusalem. Then you will delight in the sacrifices of the righteous, in burnt offerings offered whole; then bulls will be offered on your altar.

That man was transformed by speaking God's Word! At some point in his life, he had memorized Psalm 51 and now speaking the Word out loud transformed him from a hunched over beggar to a leaping hopeful joyous man with his sights again on heaven.

I must say that I was immediately challenged to learn Psalm 51. I went home and told my son, and then we both shared this story with the church. Marc read the scripture as I acted out what the man did as he spoke the amazing, powerful Logos Word of God. We then decided to learn a new verse each day until we had the entire Psalm memorized. I am not making excuses, but this is not an easy task; however, I have most of the Psalm memorized and anticipate going back to that gas station with the hope of finding that man so that I may share how he compelled me to learn Psalm 51.

The transformation that took place in that man is what happens to us as we meditate on God's Word, His truth. This world can be challenging, and life certainly comes at you fast. But I want to have the arsenal of God's Word stored up in my heart. For David stated, "Thy Word have I hid in my heart that I might not sin against you," and "thy Word is a lamp unto my feet and a light unto my path." He knew the importance of God's Word. Anyone who has experienced their spirit man rise up when hearing or speaking God's Word can attest to its power.

I will never forget that day, that man, or Psalm 51.

CHAPTER 12

Mom, Could I Pray for a Pool?

When my daughter, Jennifer, was about eight, and my son, Marc, was five, they were still sharing a bedroom and sleeping in bunk beds. I thought perhaps it was time for them to have their own bedrooms. So I shared with them that their dad and I were going to begin looking for a new apartment.

Jennifer asked, "Would it be okay to pray for a pool?"

I thought for a moment, then responded, "I don't see why not. The Lord says that if you delight in Him, He will give you the desires of your heart."

For the next several weeks, my husband and I combed through the newspaper for rentals, and we made appointments to walk through the possibilities. The whole process, as you may know, takes time.

One day, in response to a rental ad, we made an appointment to see a three-bedroom apartment on the second floor of a two-family home. The landlord was very nice; the apartment had the additional room we needed; and the location was great. After showing us the inside, the landlady said, "Now let me show you the yard." We made our way outside, and she led us to the fenced in side yard. She opened the fence door, and we looked in.

"A pool!" Jennifer screeched with joy. There inside the fence was a beautiful built in swimming pool. The landlady said we would be welcome to use the pool any time, and that it was a great location for a birthday pool party.

We lived in that second-floor apartment and enjoyed that pool for several years.

Every time I think of that day, that apartment, that pool, I think how God did exceedingly abundantly above all that Jennifer asked or could have imagined.

Now I am not saying that we can click our ruby-red slippers together and ask for whatever we want, and God will, like a big genie in the sky, make it appear. But I know that our Heavenly Father loves to bless His kids, and it has been my experience that He loves to surprise them as well with good things. To this day, when I think about Jennifer asking if she could pray for a pool, and I recall how God answered, I get giddy inside and then tear up because that was monumental.

Even now, Jennifer remembers that pool, and I am writing to remind her that it was answered prayer. Thank you, God, for your goodness and grace. You are the God who is "able to do immeasurably more than all we ask or imagine" (Ephesians 3:20).

Beautiful built in swimming pool we were
blessed to use for several years.

Photo of the church kids gathered for a photo
at a pool party.

CHAPTER 13

Money Multiplied in My Hand

We were living at that second-floor apartment with the pool. The kids were attending Crossroads Christian Academy, and I was teaching at that school. Teaching at that school was a privilege. It was also a sacrifice monetarily.

In those days, money was always tight, but during this one-month funds were exceptionally sparse. It was Sunday morning, and I was getting ready for church, and I took a look at my funds to prepare my tithe and offering. This particular Sunday was the first of the month, and rent was due. I counted my money and had just enough to pay rent. That meant no groceries for the week and no tithe and offering.

So now I had a dilemma. If I gave my tithe and offering, then I would not have enough for the rent. I would have to walk past the landlady's door to go out and come in. It is amazing to me how quickly that "voice of reason" begins to whisper, "You don't have to give your tithe. God will understand. He knows you have to pay your rent."

Over time, I have found that "voice of reason" is really the one who wars against my soul. The one who would have me compromise at every turn. Compromise is not the environment in which God moves. It is when we are obedient to do what we know is right that God moves in our lives. Obedience is better than sacrifice (1 Samuel 15:22).

So here I was standing in my kitchen with the proverbial devil on one shoulder and an angel on the other shoulder. One side told me, "God will understand. Don't give your tithe this week. Pay your rent." The other whispered, "Don't listen to him. You need to be obedient to God's Word."

I became annoyed that the enemy that wars against my soul actually engaged my emotions to get me to listen. I fired back, "Oh, you would have me withhold from God? A God who does not need my money, but says He is my Provider. You know what? I'm gonna give more. I trust and love the Lord. He has taken me out of Egypt and out of that bondage. He has set my feet on a solid rock. He has made my path straight. Regardless of the outcome, I will give."

I put my offering into an envelope, and I went to church with the kids.

Later, we arrived home from church. I got the kids settled and went to count my money thinking perhaps I could give a partial rent payment so that I could buy groceries. I counted and had $20 more than I thought I should, so I figured I must have miscounted. I counted again and had $20 more than the last time I counted. I chuckled to myself, "Come on...pay attention and count the money!" I counted again and again, $20 more than the last time. This cannot be, I thought. Why would I think that "this cannot be?" After all, God has a history of multiplying resources. Five loaves and two fish to feed more than five thousand with leftovers! He did this on more than one occasion in scripture, Matthew 14 and 15.

The jars of oil also came immediately to mind:

Elijah and the Widow at Zarephath

Sometime later the brook dried up because there had been no rain in the land. Then the word of the Lord came to him: "Go at once to Zarephath in the region of Sidon and stay there. I have directed a widow there to supply you with food." So he went to Zarephath. When he came to the town gate, a widow was there gathering sticks.

He called to her and asked, "Would you bring me a little water in a jar so I may have a drink?" As she was going to get it, he called, "And bring me, please, a piece of bread." "As surely as the Lord your God lives," she replied, "I don't have any bread—only a handful of flour in a jar and a little olive oil in a jug. I am gathering a few sticks to take home and make a meal for myself and my son, that we may eat it—and die." Elijah said to her, "Don't be afraid. Go home and do as you have said. But first make a small loaf of bread for me from what you have and bring it to me, and then make something for yourself and your son. For this is what the Lord, the God of Israel, says: 'The jar of flour will not be used up and the jug of oil will not run dry until the day the Lord sends rain on the land.'" She went away and did as Elijah had told her. So there was food every day for Elijah and for the woman and her family. For the jar of flour was not used up and the jug of oil did not run dry, in keeping with the word of the Lord spoken by Elijah. (1 Kings 1:7–16)

The Widow's Olive Oil

The wife of a man from the company of the prophets cried out to Elisha, "Your servant my husband is dead, and you know that he revered the Lord. But now his creditor is coming to take my two boys as his slaves." Elisha replied to her, "How can I help you? Tell me, what do you have in your house?" "Your servant has nothing there at all," she said, "except a small jar of olive oil." Elisha said, "Go around and ask all your neighbors for empty jars. Don't ask for just a few. Then go inside and shut the door behind you and your sons. Pour oil into all the jars, and as each is filled, put it to one side." She left him and shut the door behind her and her sons. They brought the jars to her and she kept pouring. When all the jars were full, she said to her son, "Bring me another one." But he replied, "There is not a jar left." Then the oil stopped flowing. She went and told the man of God, and he said, "Go, sell the oil and pay your debts. You and your sons can live on what is left." (2 Kings 4)

God has a history of helping those who cry out to Him in need. So why would it be so ludicrous to think that just as He multiplied the oil for those two women could He not multiply the $20s for this woman?

I counted the twenties numerous times, and each time the money in my hand multiplied. That money increased until I had rent money *and* grocery money. I know this sounds so outlandish! It really is incredible but true!

But God...multiplied fish and loaves of bread and fed over five thousand with twelve baskets leftover (Matthew 14 and 15, Mark 6, and Luke 9), directed the disciples to a fish where they pulled a coin out of its mouth to pay their taxes (Matthew 17:27), provided manna every day in the wilderness (Exodus 16), directed a raven to bring nourishment to Elijah as he sat under a tree depressed and wanting to die (1 Kings 17), spoke into existence the entire world and all the heavens (Genesis 1), owns the cattle on a thousand hills (Psalm 50:10), has unlimited resources, and is my Heavenly Father, my Provider, the God who sees me.

I gave testimony in church of God's goodness to take my very limited resources and multiply them until I had not only rent but grocery money and had paid my tithe and given extra as an offering. I told of how the $20 bills multiplied each time I recounted. My sweet friend, Angela, hollered out from behind the piano, "Why did you stop counting?" We all chuckled and gave thanks to God for who He is.

Several months after this occurred, my dear friend, Jan Rebelo, shared with me that God had multiplied money in her hand too. I looked at her wondering why didn't you give testimony? She shrugged, and I got the impression that it seemed too unbelievable.

Jan has since gone home to be with the Lord, but I remember every sweet conversation we shared and that one especially. I am grateful that one day, when I am called home, Jan and I will be able to catch up, and we can share more stories of the marvelous works of God.

Thank you, Lord, for your goodness and faithfulness.

CHAPTER 14

If Only I Could Stop Smoking, Get Rid of This Big Sin, Then I'd Have It All Together

I began smoking cigarettes when I was twelve years old. I smoked a pack of Marlboros or Newports daily for too many years. When I gave my heart to Jesus, the time came when he impressed on me the need to put this habit down.

1 Corinthians 6:19-20 states, "Do you not know that your bodies are temples of the Holy Spirit, who is in you, whom you have received from God? You are not your own; you were bought at a price. Therefore honor God with your bodies."

I wanted to get this habit out of my life. I cannot count how many times I vowed to stop, went a few days, a few weeks, or a few months. Whether it was a good day or a bad day, a wall would go up around my heart and mind, and I would beeline to the store and buy a pack of cigarettes. This was a very difficult stronghold to tear down. I would smoke one or two cigarettes and become completely disgusted with myself for not being strong enough to "just say no." I had to figure out how to address the desire to smoke before the wall went up around my conscience. I asked God to please show me.

It is so very important that we are aware of our tendencies and our old nature with its habitual thinking so that we can be sensitive to the lures of the enemy. I'd like to say that there is some easy formula for breaking the bondage in our lives, but truly it comes from transforming our minds by the Word of God. Transforming our minds will transform our heart. A transformed heart truly wants to do only those things that are pleasing to God and will push out those things that bring separation.

The Lord showed me that when I wanted to smoke, I would go off by myself. That cigarette and the desire to smoke would separate me from my family and friends. He showed me that it also separates me from Him. Sin separates. It took time and perseverance, but I have been smoke-free for over a decade. Thank you, Lord, for that deliverance!

So that *big sin* was addressed; I had finally arrived, right?

The Lord is so gracious and wise not to show us all the work that needs to be done in our lives up front, or we might become overwhelmed and lose heart that the task is too enormous, and we would walk away. Instead, He impresses on us certain areas that require transformation and shows us His Word to apply to that area so that it can be washed clean. He was gracious to give me a little bit of time to savor that victory. Then He said, "Okay, let me show you another area that requires work."

You see transformation is a process. You give your life to Jesus, and yes, at that moment, you are a new creation; however, that old man and his way of thinking needs to be transformed. Respect the process. Walk in His ways, read His Word, and adjust your life accordingly. Never forget, there is one who wars against your soul.

"Dear friends, I urge you, as foreigners and exiles, to abstain from sinful desires, which wage war against your soul" (1 Peter 2:11).

"Be alert and of sober mind. Your enemy the devil prowls around like a roaring lion looking for someone to devour" (1 Peter 5:8).

That enemy likes to try the back-door approach to see if you are still fortified in that area or if perhaps there is a crack, which can be penetrated. I had been smoke-free for several years and was traveling on business. Usually when I was going to be traveling, I would pick up a new CD so that I could worship on my way and prepare myself for the business ahead and any divine appointments.

I was on my way to Bangor, Maine, which was easily a six-hour drive from home. I was listening to a new worship CD and praising and thanking God for His abundant grace and mercy. I was traveling the highway in Maine where all you see are pine trees, highway, and moose crossing signs. Suddenly a thought entered my mind: "Wouldn't a cigarette taste good right about now? You can take the exit and buy a pack. No one knows you here."

Where in the world did that come from? Right in the middle of this worship CD, you gonna hit me with that thought? I kept driving. I got to the hotel, which would be home for the next few days and checked in. As I was heading to my room, I could hear music from the lounge. Suddenly a thought entered my mind, "Go ahead, have a few drinks. Loosen up. You don't have to be anywhere until tomorrow morning. No one knows you here. You have been working so hard and deserve some down time." I was infuriated!

Oh, so you think that you can come in through the back door? Entice me with secret sin?

The enemy loves for us to indulge in secret sin. Since that sin will then neutralize us and keep us from being transparent with God and others. You see how crafty he is to just place that thought, just whisper a suggestion. He is testing our fortitude. That is why we need to be sober and vigilant, for he seeks to devour. So what did I do? I'm glad you asked.

I entered my room, locked the door behind me, and settled in. I found a Christian radio station to set the mood. I opened the nightstand drawer and thanked the Gideons for providing a Bible. I began to thank God for who He is, then I began to pray for my church. I visualized each pew and the faces that would sit there on Sunday morning, and I prayed specifically as the Lord showed me needs. Then I prayed for my neighbors, visualizing each house and its inhabitants. I then prayed as I was led by the Spirit for the mission fields. I prayed until two in the morning for every person the Lord would bring to my mind. Then I reminded Satan that He is a liar and a cheat. He came to steal, kill, and destroy, but God came that I might have life to the fullest! He would like me to believe that momentary pleasures are worth it, but momentary pleasures bring regret, and I refuse to carry that baggage any longer.

I told him that anytime he tried to seduce me with secret sin, I would pray with all my might and praise the Creator of the universe. I set my mind on things above.

> Since, then, you have been raised with Christ, set your hearts on things above, where Christ is, seated at the right hand of God. Set your minds on things above, not on earthly things. For you died, and your life is now hidden with Christ in God. When Christ, who is your life, appears, then you also will appear with him in glory. Put to death, therefore, whatever belongs to your earthly nature. (Colossians 3:1–5)

> Therefore, as God's chosen people, holy and dearly loved, clothe yourselves with compassion, kindness, humility, gentleness and patience. Bear with each other and forgive one another if any of you has a grievance against someone. Forgive as the Lord forgave you. And over all these virtues put on love, which binds them all together in perfect unity. Let the peace of Christ rule in your hearts, since as members of one body you were called to peace. And be thankful. Let the message of Christ dwell among you richly as you teach and admonish one another with all wisdom through psalms, hymns, and songs from the Spirit, singing to God with gratitude in your hearts. And whatever you do, whether in word or deed, do it all in the name of the Lord Jesus, giving thanks to God the Father through him. (Colossians 3:12–17)

Understand that transformation is a process. So choose not to point out the speck in your brother's eye but come along side and say, "I see you're struggling. How can I help?"

It is easy to point out the outward things such as smoke and drink, but we have so much inside that is not visible. Jealousy, anger, greed, lust, to name just a few. These areas need to be addressed if we are to be made whole and healed. Let us not be so quick to judge each other. Let us with compassion press on toward the goal compelling others to do the same and let the peace of Christ rule in your heart.

CHAPTER 15

Healed from Fibromyalgia

Jeremiah 10:13 states, "But God made the earth by his power; He founded the world by his wisdom and stretched out the heavens by His understanding. When He thunders, the waters in the heavens roar; He makes clouds rise from the ends of the earth. He sends lightning with the rain and brings out the wind from his storehouses."

I suffered from fibromyalgia for over twenty years. The pain many times took me to the brink of suicide; I just wanted to be free from pain. Periodically I would experience a reprieve from the pain a day or two, sometimes a week, pain free. God would make it clear to me that he was fully in control of this illness in my life, and He was allowing it because it was beneficial.

God has impressed the word *beneficial* on me for several different circumstances in my life. I am just beginning to understand that word in the context of all things working together for the good of them that are called according to His purpose (Romans 8:28).

On many occasions, if I summoned the strength and wherewithal to go to church on Sunday, even though the pain was unbearable, and the enemy was telling me to stay home by using the God-will-understand reasoning. as soon as I entered into worship, I was pain free. I could worship the Lord in the freedom that comes with His presence. "For where the Spirit of the Lord is, there is liberty" (1 Corinthians 3:17).

Pain would resume as I exited the church, but again my Heavenly Father was allowing this in my life to bring about healing and wholeness. It was beneficial.

I went to numerous prayer services, moving forward when the call went out for anyone in need of healing. Nothing changed. Over time, I thought, "Why go forward?" But then, hope would whisper, "Where there is Christ, there is hope. Do not lose the expectation of God's intervention."

I think that it is human nature to start to give up after days, weeks, months, and then years go by, and you have not received that for which you've been praying. You start to lose hope. Yes, there is that little glimmer of expectation, but it is not as bright as it once was. I know positionally I am healed. I know I will receive a new body one day when mortality puts on immortality. I don't want to just accept that this is my life, a life of pain, but at the same time, I want to be thankful that I even have a life. I want to expect a work of God because all things are possible with God, but I want to live in the place that it is well with my soul.

The ladies of our church participated in an annual retreat with women from southern New England, and we all descended on the Host Hotel in Sturbridge Village, Massachusetts, for three glorious days. We would leave the church parking lot on Thursday afternoon and arrive home Saturday evening. We checked into our rooms, got a bite to eat, and then picked up our packets of information at the front desks. These packets gave us information about the speakers and mini-seminars going on all weekend. *I loved retreat!* Of course, trying to get away from work and family responsibilities was no small task. So by the time we arrived, I was usually exhausted from all the coordination efforts it took to get there. So that bite to eat and sweet fellowship with my friends was just what I needed to refuel. I just loved getting together with women of God. Worshipping together and rubbing shoulders with people of like faith is truly heaven!

This particular retreat occurred the weekend of my birthday. My sweet friend, Sandy, and I celebrated our birthdays at the same time, and she had also come to this retreat. Thursday night was the kickoff. The speaker was wonderful, and worship is amazing when you are in a room filled with hundreds of spirit-filled women. The workshops scheduled for Friday looked informative and interesting. I really appreciated all of the women who took the time to prepare and present. I always took away something to chew on from the workshops.

Friday night came, and we finished our dinner and headed to the conference room to assemble for worship. The music saturated the entire room. I stopped singing to listen to the sounds of the voices all around me worshipping the Creator of the universe, Adonah, Possessor of Heaven and earth, Jesus, the Lover of my soul.

The Lord whispered to me, "Step out and be healed." The wonder of a God, who set the earth on its axis and placed the stars in the sky yet bows down to whisper to me personally, is too much to fathom with my human mind.

I am hoping at this moment you're saying, "Well, did you? Did you step out?"

The answer is *yes*. I was mid row, so I had to quietly excuse myself to get to the aisle. Then I just stood there in the aisle and worshipped. As I worshipped there in the middle of the aisle, an incredible warmth washed over me and dispelled all of my pain. It was such an intimate moment. My Savior, my Lord, my Kinsman Redeemer, the Lover of my soul was with me.

The warmth washed over me, and I was grateful for a reprieve from the pain. God once again let me know that He was in control. The music faded; the crowd of women began to disperse. I sat down drinking in this incredible encounter with the One True and Living God. I did not want this moment to end. Angela, my pastor's wife and dearest friend, sat down next to me for a while. After some time, she whispered to me, "They have cake upstairs to celebrate Sandy and your birthdays."

I turned to her and said, "Just a little while longer."

We eventually made it back to our room to have our celebratory cake and mingle with ladies from other area churches. I enjoyed feeling pain free for the rest of the weekend and hanging out with the ladies. What a wonderful birthday present!

We all made it home safely and joyfully attended our local church the next day. I was still riding the pain-free wave and cherished every moment of that experience.

A few days went by. A few weeks went by. Yes, even a few years went by, I was still pain free! I was sleeping through the night and waking up refreshed. Migraines were a thing of the past. I don't think I even had a headache. Could this be it? Could this be more than a very long reprieve? Could I indeed be healed? He did whisper, "Step out and be healed," and I was obedient to do so.

I allowed more time to pass before I gave testimony. I certainly did not want to proclaim that God healed me, unless I was absolutely without a doubt 100 percent certain. I made an appointment to see the specialist so that this doctor could document that I was healed from this dreadful disease. It just so happened that the day of my appointment at the medical building, I walked past a sandwich board that advertised a study that was currently in process. "The power of prayer," talk about timing!

I was escorted to the exam room. A young lady entered, who was completing her clinicals, and asked if she could examine me. I explained to her that I was here to document that God healed me from fibromyalgia, and I would like her to press the previous points of pain to prove it. This female doctor methodically pressed each location that in the past had dropped me to my knees, but now had no effect.

I explained that my Heavenly Father whispered to me to come out and be healed. There was no going forth to be prayed over, no special prayer meeting, nothing like that. It was an intimate moment between me and my Abba Father. I added that prayer is a wonderful thing, but to whom you pray determines the results.

I shared with her my faith in Jesus Christ as my Lord and Savior and how I have been adjusting my life according to His Word for years. I shared how He has made me whole and continues to heal those dark corners in my heart that no one knows about.

I don't know if that female Hindu doctor was curious enough to seek Jesus. I do know that in my medical file it is documented that I no longer suffer from fibromyalgia because I was healed by the power of God through His Son, Jesus.

I am pain free to this very day! Thank you, Jesus!

CHAPTER 16

Hope Deferred Makes the Heart Sick

P roverbs 13:12 states "Hope deferred makes the heart sick." Anyone who has ever hoped for a change in a loved one or in themselves can confirm this to be true. As the cycle continues, hope fades.

I was brought to that place of fading hope when the pain of fibromyalgia gripped me. It was relentless; the migraines were crippling; and at times, I wanted to end it all. But the Creator of the universe would speak to my heart, "Where there is Christ, there is hope."

That whisper would cause me to focus again on truth:

"My hope comes from Him" (Psalms 62:5).

"And in His Word I put my hope" (Psalms 130:5).

"There is surely a future hope for you" (Psalms 23:18).

"He has plans to give you a hope and a future" (Jeremiah 29:11).

"And therefore I have hope" (Lamentations 3:21).

"Be joyful in hope and patient in affliction" (Romans 12:12).

"For in this life we have hope in Christ" (1 Corinthians 15:19).

"And your endurance is inspired by hope" (1 Thessalonians 1:3).

"We rest in the hope of eternal life" (Titus 1:2).

"And while we wait for the blessed hope" (Titus 2:13).

"We have this hope as an anchor" (Hebrews 6:19).

"If we hold unswervingly to the hope we profess" (Hebrews 10:23).

Okay, so there is the *if...if* we hold unswervingly...So there must be opportunity to let go, give up, or not hold unswervingly. This system in this world will give you all the opportunities to give up or let go. Do not do it!

Well-meaning people will suggest you give up. Your own heart may say it is too much, and you cannot take the hurt any more. What you see with your eyes and reason in your mind will tell you that it no longer makes sense to hope. But what does God's Word say?

Job 13:15 says, "Though He slay me, yet will I hope."

Hope in what? The unchanging, infallible word of God. The unchanging word that defines you and me. We need to hold unswervingly to the hope we profess; we need to meditate on God's Word so that life can be breathed back into us. Jesus made the blind to see, the lame to walk, the mute to speak, and the deaf to hear. He healed the sick and raised the dead. That is what He did for me. I was a dead man walking until He breathed life-His Word into me.

You see if we keep reading Proverbs 13:12, we see a contrast. Hope deferred does make the heart sick, but a longing fulfilled is a tree of life!

What longing? The longing to belong and to be loved.

The world today is fascinated by zombies and the walking dead. No wonder, they have no life! There is a famine in the land. People no longer read, meditate and apply God's word. But you are a chosen people, a holy priesthood, a people belonging to God that you may declare the praises of Him who has called you out of darkness and into His wonderful light!

Each day, each hour, each moment, we are faced with a choice. Choose hope! Choose the giver of life! Be patient in affliction and joyful in hope! Become well acquainted with the Sustainer of life! Become well acquainted with his unchanging word.

You cannot place hope in your job, your bank account, your 401K, or others. All of these things can change and may let you down.

However there is One who changest not, like shifting shadows.

I pray you put your hope in the person of Jesus Christ, who is the Word made flesh. For heaven and earth will pass away, but the word of the Lord stands FOREVER!

CHAPTER 17

As Long As It Depends on You, Live at Peace

We bought our first home in the year 2000. It was built by a sweet Italian man who lived there with his family his entire life. When he and his wife passed away, their children put it on the market.

It was a bit run down but had great "bones." We closed on December 18, 2000, cleaned like crazy, moved in, decorated for the holiday, and had our first Christmas with the whole family seven days later in this house on December 25!

Our family consisted of my husband, Kiki; my daughter, Jennifer; my son, Marco; and five beagles. The beagles were hunting dogs who lived outside in a kennel. When spring came, our neighbors in the corner house and the house behind us began to complain to the town officials about the kennel and our dogs.

Initially, the dog warden paid us a visit due to reports of us treating the dogs inhumanly. The dog warden found the dogs to be in excellent health, full of life, and tremendously friendly. She asked if they barked or howled much. We informed her that they did bark from time to time if something were to come into the yard, or they heard strange noises.

The next official to visit was the building inspector, who was concerned about reports that a structure had been erected on our land, but he had no permit on file. We explained that this kennel was not a permanent structure and that we had moved it from our old address. Then came the various police visits. The neighbor in the back stated that he was becoming anxious about the dog kennel butting up against his property. He went and got a doctor's note stating that he was experiencing anxiety.

In the movies, when someone moves into a neighborhood, the neighbors bring pie and introduce themselves. So I figured that I would put a spin on that idea. I baked my award-winning (blue ribbon at the Berlin Fair) carrot cakes, and I went and visited my neighbors to introduce myself. I provided my telephone number to each of these neighbors and let them know that I wanted to be a good neighbor, but perhaps we got off to a rocky start. I asked them to please call me if there was an issue so that I could resolve it without involving town officials.

The corner neighbor informed me that my house looked like a "junk house," and my vehicles were junk. I swallowed, took a breath, and responded, "Please know that it is my desire to be a good neighbor. My intent is to make repairs to the house over time and refurbish it. My cars are not junk. They are in perfect working order, just a few years older than yours."

The neighbor in the back took my carrot cake and said, "Okay."

The neighbor on the corner continued to call the police and complain about various things. The dogs' barking, my daughter's alarm clock being too loud, etc. He began to take photos of our home, our vehicles, our activities. I can still see him and his wife in my mind's eye peeping out the front door or side window with their camera. The police informed me that he was keeping a log of our activity and when our dogs barked: 11:00 p.m., dogs barked thirty seconds; 3:00 a.m., dogs barked fifteen seconds; 7:00 a.m., dogs barked forty-five seconds. This continued for over eighteen months.

I came home from work one fall day and pulled my car into the driveway. The corner neighbor came out and began yelling at me that we were blowing leaves onto his lawn. I assured him that we were doing nothing of the sort, nor would we ever. I shared with him that the wind has a tendency to blow in his direction, and that I have had McDonald's wrappers and various other items blow onto my lawn. Soon the police showed up, and the man kept yelling at me. The policeman said to me that if this man is yelling in this manner with the police present, he can only imagine how he behaves when the police are not present. So what do you do in this situation? This neighbor would not listen to reason. My husband was on the warpath. My emotions really wanted to take me for a ride. I wanted to live at peace, but peace seemed out of my reach.

I am reminded that in God's Word, Jesus says, "In this world we will have troubles of many kinds, but take heart for I have overcome the world."

Okay, so this is trouble. Father, what would you have me to do?

I am reminded of God's Word, "But I tell you, love your enemies and pray for those who persecute you."

So I determined that I would pray for this man and his wife and whatever their circumstances were. As I prayed for this man and woman, I was overwhelmed with sympathy and compassion for them. I watched this man take meticulous care of his postage-stamp-sized lawn and prayed for God to move on them. They had need of salvation. They need to know your love, Lord. For if they truly knew Your love, it would change their lives.

I continued this course of action for months. I came home one day to find the neighbors in back, blowing an air horn and swearing at the dogs. I went to their house and knocked on the door. The gentleman answered, and I asked if he could please refrain from this activity. He said he had no idea what I was talking about, and so it became clear that reasoning with this man was not a possibility.

It seemed as though I was not going to find peace in my new home. The police were a constant presence, checking on complaints regarding our dogs barking. I found the neighbor in back had put up a device that made a high-pitched sound, causing the dogs to become restless and bark. We put bark collars on them until we could have this device removed. We had to hire a lawyer to represent us because the two neighbors wanted the dogs removed from the property.

We won the case, but nothing really changed. My husband was becoming more infuriated with the neighbors and the police who now came to check on every complaint. Just when I thought perhaps I should sell the house and move, I came home one day to find my corner neighbor blowing the leaves off of my front lawn. I pulled my car into the driveway and said, "Hello."

Don said to me, "The leaf truck is coming around for their last pick up, and I thought I would clear your leaves in time for that pick-up." He added, "I want to be a good neighbor."

We chatted for a little while, and I found out that his wife was struggling with cancer. I told him that I was very sorry to hear that news, and that I would remember her and his family in my prayers.

Winter came, and with it, an onslaught of snowstorms. One day, during a snowstorm, my daughter came running downstairs, yelling, "Mom, Mom look out the window! You're never gonna believe it!" So I ran to the window and looked out.

In the midst of this blizzard, my corner neighbor was out with his snowblower clearing my sidewalk with a smile on his face, waving. He not only cleared my snow but went on to clear my other neighbor's sidewalk also. It was an amazing moment. We were laughing and crying and rejoicing and thanking God for His Word and His wisdom.

"When a man's ways are pleasing to the Lord, he makes even his enemies live at peace with him" (Proverbs 16:7).

"If it is possible, as long as it depends on you, live at peace with everyone" (Romans 12:18).

Amen?

Oh, by the way, I believe his wife is cancer free. I do not know the details. They sold their house and moved away. I only know that I see her from time to time at the grocery store, and she looks great!

CHAPTER 18

No Harm Will Come Near Your Tent

When my children, Jennifer and Marco, were young, we liked to go camping. My in-laws invited us to stay at a campground near the Canadian border one year during the summer. We accepted their invitation and packed our camping gear and headed off for a week at this marvelous campground. I was looking forward to rest and relaxation, and the kids were looking forward to socializing and swimming with the other kids staying at that campground.

As soon as we arrived, I began to set up our tent and get our things organized. The kids ran off to explore. It was a great day. The sunshine was warm, and the kids were able to swim most of the day. I was looking forward to an entire week of taking it easy.

Around 10:00 p.m., we settled down for the evening in our tent. It did not take long for the kids to fall into a deep sleep. I pulled out my Bible and began to read, thanking God for the opportunity to come to this campground and for the privilege of freely reading His Word.

I turned to Psalm 91 and read...

> Whoever dwells in the shelter of the Most High will rest in the shadow of the Almighty. I will say of the Lord, "He is my refuge and my fortress, my God, in whom I trust." Surely he will save you

from the fowler's snare and from the deadly pestilence. He will cover you with his feathers, and under his wings you will find refuge; His faithfulness will be your shield and rampart. You will not fear the terror of night, nor the arrow that flies by day, nor the pestilence that stalks in the darkness, nor the plague that destroys at midday. A thousand may fall at your side, ten thousand at your right hand, but it will not come near you. You will only observe with your eyes and see the punishment of the wicked. If you say, "The Lord is my refuge," and you make the Most High your dwelling, no harm will overtake you, no disaster will come near your tent. For he will command his angels concerning you to guard you in all your ways; they will lift you up in their hands, so that you will not strike your foot against a stone. You will tread on the lion and the cobra; you will trample the great lion and the serpent. "Because he loves me," says the Lord, "I will rescue him; I will protect him, for he acknowledges my name. He will call on me, and I will answer him; I will be with him in trouble, I will deliver him and honor him. With long life I will satisfy him and show him my salvation."

Do you remember the butterflies you would get in your tummy when you were smitten or had a crush on someone, and that someone would look your way or speak to you? You would get giddy, and your face beamed as the corners of your mouth could not help but turn up to create a smile.

That is how I felt when I read this Psalm and came to verse 10; no disaster will come near your tent. Thank you, Lord, that you would give me a scripture that speaks of being in a tent while I am camping. Thank you that no disaster will come near my tent. You are such an amazing God, and you speak to me here and now in my tent about a tent. I just *love that!*

I opened up a bag of chips and began to munch and meditate on this Psalm and what my Heavenly Father was teaching me about how He protects His kids; His faithfulness will be my shield and rampart. I do not have to fear the terror of the night or the pestilence that stalks in the darkness.

I was drinking in these verses and resting in knowing that the Lord says, "Because he loves me, I will rescue him. I will protect him because he acknowledges my name." I sat back and made that personal. Because I love you, Lord, you will rescue me. You will protect me because I acknowledge your name; therefore, I do not need to fear the terror of the night or the pestilence that stalks in the darkness.

The dictionary defines the following:

Shield and rampart, a protective barrier: bulwark, a broad embankment raised as a fortification and usually surmounted by a parapet, a wall-like ridge (as of rock fragments, earth, or debris)

Pestilence: a suddenly fatal epidemic disease such as the bubonic plague, a pernicious evil influence or agent.

So pestilence can affect both the physical and the spiritual man. Interesting. But I am safe because of His faithfulness which is a shield and rampart, a raised fortification. Hmmm…

So now, it was after midnight, and I needed to get some sleep, so I put away the bag of chips and settled into my sleeping bag. I awoke in the middle of the night to the sound of my son, Marco, saying in a quivering soft voice, "Mom, please wake up. Mom, pleeeeaaase wake up."

I opened my eyes and saw a skunk sniffing the sleeve of Marco's sweatshirt. Marco happened to be wearing a sweatshirt with a single white stripe down each sleeve. I still wonder if that skunk thought Marco was a skunk because of those stripes. I slowly picked my head off of my pillow to find a second skunk at the foot of his sleeping bag looking into a mirror and rubbing his greasy nose on it as if he was seeing another skunk. I moved my leg, and that skunk looked at me and turned his backside just a little as if to convey to me that I should not make any sudden moves.

Just then, the bag of chips crinkled, and I saw yet another skunk in that bag crunching on my chips! I quietly began to nudge Jennifer, who was lying in the middle of Marco and me. I said softly, "Wake up, Jen, but do not move. There are skunks in the tent, and we need to carefully exit."

I told Marco that Jennifer would quietly and slowly exit the tent, and then he could slide close to me and do the same. We all slowly and without incident were able to exit the tent. I woke my in-laws and asked if we could stay in their camper for the night. I got Jennifer and Marco tucked in, and they fell back to sleep. I, on the other hand, stayed very much awake sitting on the bench at the window of the RV to keep an eye on the tent, praying that these skunks would not spray our belongings. I watched and prayed until dawn, which is when these skunks finally left our tent; all five of them!

I thanked God that not a single skunk sprayed our belongings or any of us. I questioned why were these skunks able to gain entry? I read in Psalm 91 that no harm will overtake us, and no disaster would come near our tent. God responded quietly to my spirit, "Were you overtaken or merely inconvenienced?"

Let me talk to you for a moment about inconveniences. I call it life. Life has a way of coming at you fast and hitting you when you least expect. It catches you off guard and stresses you out with last-minute changes to plans. It may come in the form of flat tires, misplaced cell phones, or the baby pooping all the way up his or her back. We live in a fast-paced world.

"Because he loves me I will rescue him. I will protect him because he acknowledges my name." Hmmm…this would mean that we would have a need to be rescued and a need to be protected. Lord, I am so very grateful for your promise. I know that nothing catches you off guard. Help us, Lord, when life comes at us to remember, we can dwell in the shelter of the Most High and rest in the shadow of the Almighty. Let us in those times to take a deep breath and gain perspective.

I spent the rest of the morning sweeping out our tent and sanitizing to remove the smell of the salty chips, which I was informed was probably what drew them into the tent in the first place. I was surprised that they were able to unzip the zippers of the tent to gain entry. I was also surprised to find that their poops look like crushed

Oreo cookies. A few of the campers told me that the skunks had become a problem at this campground because many people actually feed them, and so they are not exceptionally afraid of humans, and they forage around the campsites for food.

Since the skunks were able to unzip the zippers that secured the entry of the tent, I was determined to secure that entry point with safety pins. I would pin all three zippers with one pin so that they could not be unzipped.

The second night, the skunks caught me off guard by coming just before dusk and gaining entry to our tent before I could get inside and secure the zippers. Again, the kids slept in my in-law's camper, and I watched and prayed. The skunks did not spray, and just like the first night, they left at the crack of dawn.

Once again, I swept and sanitized.

Prior to evening three, I placed a kerosene lantern at the entry of our tent to deter any early birds, I mean skunks, from getting close to the entrance of our tent and secured the zippers with a safety pin just in case. No sign of skunks. Thank you, Lord!

I was looking forward to getting a good night sleep. We all got tucked in, and I secured the zippers, and it did not take long for all of us to fall into a wonderful deep slumber. About 3:00 a.m., there was tugging at the zipper, then scratching on our tent, then digging right by my head. Those skunks were running up the sides of the tent and head butting the entry. For a good long time, they kept up this behavior. Then as quickly as they ascended on our tent, they left. It was dawn! Hallelujah! We were actually able to stay in our tent all night.

My Heavenly Father saved me from the fowler's snare and from the deadly pestilence. The three of us emerged from our tent in the morning to find what looked like crushed Oreo cookies, which were skunk poops, all around our tent. The Lord reminded me of verse 14: "Because he loves me," says the Lord, "I will rescue him. I will protect him, for he acknowledges my name."

It has been my experience that just like we use teaching moments for our children, our Heavenly Father also uses teaching moments. He is Adoniah, Possessor of heaven and earth. He can cause the sun to stand still for Joshua, calm the wind and the waves for the disciples, make it rain, and hold back the rain for Elijah. He does as He pleases to accomplish His will.

Certainly He was not caught off guard by those pesky skunks. Not at all. I think He had a twinkle in his eye and a little smirk on His glorious face when He determined to allow them entry into our tent.

I want to dwell in the shelter of the Most High and take refuge in the shadow of the Almighty. To stay in someone's shadow, you must stay close. That is where I want to be. I want to take refuge in His shadow. Refuge from the unexpected, from the deadly pestilence, you fill in the blank. I want His name on my lips and His word in my heart.

"He will call on me, and I will answer him; I will be with him in trouble, I will deliver him and honor him. With long life I will satisfy him and show him my salvation" (Psalm 91:15–16).

This is God's Word, his unchanging Word. Stand on it today for whatever has entered your life unexpectedly. His faithfulness will be your shield and rampart.

"You will not fear the terror of night, nor the arrow that flies by day, nor the pestilence that stalks in the darkness, nor the plague that destroys at midday. A thousand may fall at your side, ten thousand at your right hand, but it will not come near you" (Psalm 91:5–7).

This Psalm speaks of a twenty-four-hour period, night, day, and midday. He is our ever-present help in times of trouble.

Every time I read Psalm 91, I am reminded of those skunks. Every time I see skunks I am reminded of Psalm 91. What an incredible teacher! We were victorious over the skunks!

No harm will come near your tents (Psalm 91).

No harm, but there may be inconveniences! Amen?

CHAPTER 19

Do Not Hold So Tightly the Things of This World

I worked at a pizza restaurant as a waitress for many years. Friday nights were my busy nights as the single waitress to serve the entire dining room.

I would keep my tips in a basket under the counter near the soda fountain station. There was a dining room side and a pizza house side to this restaurant.

One night, I went over to the pizza side for food that was going to be coming out of the oven for one of my tables. While standing behind the counter, I looked through the glass to see one of the staff taking money out of my tip basket. The person was pretty slick. They went to the soda machine and while filling their cup with soda, dipped into my tip basket.

I could not believe this person, with whom I worked for a number of years was stealing from me! I then found myself constantly checking every time this person moved toward the area near my tip basket. I tried to figure out a new location for that basket, but behind that counter was really the only place.

I became consumed with *my* money in *my* basket. I began to lose focus on what I was doing and began forgetting orders and failed to deliver salads prior to meals. I was becoming consumed with guarding *my* money.

The Lord gently reminded me that it was not *my* money. He has given me health and breath and ability. "See how tightly you are holding to this little bit of cash, and how it is bringing you anxiety? See how your focus has changed from looking upon me with thankfulness to looking out for your 'stuff?' Do you think that I am not able to watch over you and care for you? Do you think I am not able to see this situation? Hold lightly to the things of this world, like money and things," which have no eternal value.

So I listened to my Heavenly Father; I relinquished my basket of tips into His hand, which brought peace and rest into my mind, life, and work. I no longer had to guard what was mine but knew that God could certainly take care of what was His.

This principle is practiced with regards to all of my, I mean, His possessions. My car is truly His car. My home is truly His home. This attitude causes me to be a good steward of the resources He loans to me. When someone loans an item to you, at some point, you must give it back, which causes you to take better care of that item while it is in your possession. And so this should be our attitude toward all that God provides/loans us in this world.

"For every animal of the forest is mine, and the cattle on a thousand hills. I know every bird in the mountains, and the insects in the fields are mine. If I were hungry I would not tell you, for the world is mine, and all that is in it" (Psalm 50:10–12).

CHAPTER 20

Angels Unaware

Do not forget to show hospitality to strangers, for by so doing some, people have shown hospitality to angels without knowing it.

At 2:00 a.m., on January 4, 1996, I received a telephone call. "Your mother's dead" the voice on the other end of the line stated. Having been aroused out of a deep sleep, I tried to make sense of that statement. "What?" I responded.

"Your mother's dead" the voice repeated.

"If this is some kind of joke, it is not funny. Who is this?" I questioned.

"It's Patrick. I am sorry to have to tell you that your mother is dead. She sat down on the sofa and asked for a drink of water. By the time, I got back to her she was no longer breathing. I pushed on her chest, and she just exhaled and slumped over. I called right away for the medics, who tried to resuscitate her, then took her by ambulance to the hospital."

Not at that moment but through this experience, the fact that all my mom could do was let out her final breath or exhale, struck me, and stayed with me. God gives us our breath, we can only exhale. Needless to say, my adrenaline was pumping. Immediately I started to create the list of "to-dos" in my head. I called my brother and shared the news with him. He rushed over, and we began to make plans. We called our sister, and she began to look for flights from California to Florida.

We had just celebrated New Years, and I had spoken to my mom by telephone on New Year's Day. She had recently moved to Port St. Lucie, Florida, where she was enjoying the warmth of Florida temperatures.

Here in New England, we were all hunkered down due to an impending blizzard. My brother and I determined that we could drive to Port St. Lucie, and my sister could fly in from her home in California. My husband would stay at home to care for our children.

Steven and I headed out at 4:00 a.m. the next morning. To this day, I am so very grateful that my brother took the first shift of driving since we had to venture through New York and New Jersey during the first phase of that blizzard.

During the first leg of that trip, we reminisced. Looking back on all the crazy times good and bad that we had experienced together. Before you know it, we were entering Virginia, and the Nor'Easter was now behind us as we traveled toward a warmer climate.

We pulled off the highway to get a little shut eye. We switched positions, since it would be my turn to drive next. I don't think I slept more than twenty minutes before my eyes popped open and a new burst of adrenaline pumped. I started the car and headed South. We drove all the way to Georgia, just above Jacksonville, Florida, before stopping to get a bite to eat and calling our sister and Patrick to let them know our location and estimated ETA.

We paid the check, filled the gas tank, and headed to Port St. Lucie, Florida.

As we drove over the Jacksonville, Florida, line we saw a sign which read, "376 miles to Miami." I looked at my brother and said, "Aren't you glad we're not going to Miami?" We both nodded in agreement and drove on.

If you have never driven I-95 south through Florida, let me share that these signs stating how many more miles to Miami are a regular occurrence. We had an estimated five-hour drive from Jacksonville to Port St. Lucie and passed numerous signs, each informing us the number of miles remaining until we reached Miami. The sign was now reading "150 miles to Miami." I looked at my brother and said, "Maybe we are going to Miami."

Along the highway, we began to see a number of abandoned cars and joked that those people must have just given up. The journey was too much, too far, too many signs, and so they just pulled to the side of the road and gave up the ghost.

As we got closer to Port St. Lucie, I reminded Steven, who was now driving, that Patrick told us not to take exit A. We were to take exit B. It was a relief when we began to see signs for Port St. Lucie. We were almost there and had made really good time considering we had to travel through that Nor'Easter back in New England.

We drove past exit A and anticipated taking exit B for Port St. Lucie. But after a good amount of time had past, and we finally were seeing the next exit, it became increasingly apparent that there was no exit B.

"Thanks, Patrick," Steven and I both yelled out in stereo. We made the quick decision to take the very next exit and double back. The very next exit did not come very quickly, but when it did, we took it. We drove for a good long time, waiting for a right-hand turn, so that we could double back. We could see lights ahead and figured that we were coming up to a mall. Excited to finally see life again we began to hoot and holler like little kids who were taking the lead in a ball game. As we drew closer, something very different appeared.

This was not a mall. The gates were high and fortified with barbed wire. This was some type of correctional facility. Looking on the map today, I can identify it as Martin Correctional Facility.

Let me take a moment to remind those who are reading and thinking why don't you use your GPS or your cell phone, that this was January 1996 and cell phones and navigation devices have not yet come on the scene or were still considered an extravagance. We still had dial up internet. If we had a map, we would have known that a left turn off the highway would have been a better option since it would have placed us onto the Florida's Turnpike fairly quickly and back up to Port St. Lucie. But we had no map, no phone, no navigation device, and I feared in time if we could not find civilization that we would have no more gas.

Have you ever been in that position of expectation and then complete let down? Since giving my life to Jesus, I tend to be a cheerleader. You know the type of person who always finds a silver lining or the upside of a story? I am a glass half full…actually a glass three-fourths full kind of person.

However, at this moment, coming up to this correctional center with no one in sight was the final component to this trip that put me over the edge. I am sure my lack of sleep and lack of a good meal played a role in my emotions overtaking me, but I began to cry and make statements like "we are *never* gonna get there!"

It was at that moment that my brother really stepped up to comfort me. He said, "We'll get there. We just got detoured. We'll get there." My brother, Steven, was such a rock at that time.

You may be on a journey you had not anticipated. It may have come upon you suddenly. It may be taking longer than you anticipated to reach your destination. It may be a season in your life that is way more difficult that you can handle at this juncture. You may have experienced a wrong turn that is now costing you unexpected time, money, and resources.

Let me encourage you to turn toward heaven and cry out to God. He will answer. He desires for you to turn to Him. He desires to comfort you and give you wisdom for the situation. Stand firm. The Lord will see you through.

We finally arrived at mom's condo.

Patrick was throwing his hands in the air, crying, "I can't believe it. I can't believe it!"

My sister was pretty wound up asking us why it took so long for us to arrive. Susan had the task of signing the death certificate, and that stress and emotion seemed to be taking a toll.

Steven and I made our way into the house, and I began to assess what needed to happen, and I began to make a list of "to dos" in my head to walk us all through this difficult time. The first thing we needed was a life insurance policy…if it existed. We asked Patrick where mom kept her documents and bills. Patrick pointed to a secretary-style desk. Looking through the sparse documents in this desk, it became immediately clear that producing a life insurance may be a problem.

As soon as we announced that there was no policy in this desk, Patrick stated that he has no money and then began throwing his hands in the air, crying, "I can't believe it. I can't believe it." I assured Patrick that we were not interested in taking his money but had to come up with a means to get mom buried. I asked if mom kept bills in any other location. Patrick pointed to a bedroom closet.

I opened the closet door to find numerous brown paper bags filled with bills, receipts, and miscellaneous papers. Susan made the decision, although Steven and I thought it premature, to begin calling our relatives to see if they could assist with the cost of Mom's burial.

Steven and I prayed and asked the Lord to please come into this situation and direct us and walk us through this process and then began the arduous task of looking at each piece of paper within each paper bag. I could hear Susan on the phone with various relatives and based on her side of the conversation, it seemed that no one was going to provide funds for mom's burial.

I came upon a policy payment booklet stub. I got giddy, thinking this could be it! I called the number. Thankfully back in 1996, automation was not the norm, so a real person answered the call.

"May I help you?" asked the voice on the other end of the phone.

"Yes, I hope so," I replied, "I am calling regarding my insurance policy," and I provided the policy number. There was a pause as she looked up the policy.

"I am sorry, Mrs. Brown, but that policy was canceled last year for nonpayment."

My heart sank, "Okay, thank you."

At that moment, everything felt like it was closing in on me. Where are we going to get the money we need to give our mom a proper burial, Lord?

The Lord quieted my heart and directed me back to the paper bags to finish the task. It took hours to look at every piece of paper and every receipt in those bags. Then in the very last bag and the very last document at the very bottom of that bag was a Guardian Life Insurance policy payment receipt. If active, this policy would provide $5,000 for our mom's burial.

I dialed the number and awaited an answer.

"Guardian Life Insurance. How may I help you?" asked the friendly voice.

I took a deep breath and asked, "I'd like to know when my next payment is due please."

"Okay, let's see. Oh, Mrs. Brown, your payment is not due until March 30."

Suddenly, my heart started to beat out of my chest. "So this policy is in good standing and active?" I questioned.

"Yes, Mrs. Brown, this account is active," the woman stated.

"Could you please check again to be sure?" I pressed.

"Yes, ma'am, I have double-checked, Mrs. Brown, and your next payment is not due until March 30. Your policy is active."

With great relief, I stated, "I'd like to report a death." There was silence on the other end. I continued, "My mother passed away two days ago from a massive heart attack. I am her daughter. My brother, sister, and I are here in Florida for her burial. Please let me know what needs to be done to cash out this policy."

Thank you, Lord! We have $5,000! Now to meet with the funeral director!

We were able to get a meeting right away with a funeral representative, Richard. We walked into his office and sat down. The notepad at the corner of his desk immediately caught my eye. It had a smiley face and stated, "Smile, Jesus loves you."

As soon as I saw this notepad, I knew the Lord had sent Richard to help us through the details of our mom's burial. Richard informed us that Mom had purchased a package that selected her plot, casket, and other details. Unfortunately, she only made a few payments, but at least, we knew what her desires were for burial.

Patrick continued to throw his arms in the air, crying, "I can't believe it, I can't believe it!"

My sister, brother, and I shared with the funeral director that mom had a $5,000 life insurance policy through Guardian Insurance. I informed the director that my mom is with Jesus, and we are merely burying the tent of her body; we would very much like to bury her in the plot she selected, but we would need to scale back on the rest of the package.

Richard thanked us for being so candid, explaining that many times, people overspend during this time of grief, then struggle to pay the bill. Richard took out the document with the itemized listing of charges and began to cross off items not required. "Disinfecting the body, $600. We can cross this off," Richard continued. "The casket, we can take off. I think I have something much cheaper." Richard revised the package to make it affordable and still give our mom a proper burial.

We were able to give our mom a proper burial, and we all traveled back to our respective homes. Over the next few months, I filed the required paperwork for my mom's final tax return and finalized the balance of her documents.

I decided to call Richard to thank him for all of his help in bringing the cost of my mom's burial to a manageable number. I called and asked to speak to Richard. The person who answered stated that no one by that name works here. I explained that several months ago, Richard was assigned to be the funeral director for my mom's burial. I added that he was tremendously helpful, and I wanted to thank him. The woman restated, "No one by that name works here."

At that time, the Lord impressed on me, "Angels unaware."

The scripture states, "Do not forget to show hospitality to strangers, for by so doing some people have shown hospitality to angels without knowing it" (Hebrews 13:2, NIV).

"Be not forgetful to entertain strangers: for thereby some have entertained angels unawares" (Hebrews 13:2, KJV).

I am so very grateful for Richard. Thank you, Lord, for sending him!

CHAPTER 21

Excellent, Incredible, Amazing

When my son, Marco, was a teenager, it was determined that he would need jaw surgery to align his lower jaw. The time came for his surgery, and we went to the hospital, and the nurses prepped Marco for his surgery. As he lay in his bed, waiting to be wheeled into the operating room, I leaned toward him and asked, "Do you want to pray?"

"Yes!" Marco responded.

We prayed and asked the Lord to guide the surgeons' hands. We prayed for a full recovery for Marco and asked to hear the words *excellent, incredible,* and *amazing* concerning Marco's recovery.

When we finished praying and opened our eyes, we saw Marco's surgical team assembled at the foot of his bed. They asked if he was ready. He nodded, and they wheeled him away. The surgery took several hours, but finally the nurse informed me that Marco was in recovery. I quickly got up to go see him. His face and lips were so swollen. The doctor stepped in and informed me that Marco would continue to swell over the next twenty-four hours.

"Can his lips get any bigger?" I half questioned in disbelief.

Just then, Marco whispered, "Waaater."

I asked the nurse if Marco could have water, and she provided me with a half cup of cold water and a straw. I gently placed it to his lips, and he sucked it all down.

"Mooore," he whispered.

I asked the nurse if it was okay to give him more. She nodded and filled the cup for me.

Marco stayed in the hospital over the next few days until the doctors were confident that he was ready for home care. I had gotten his room ready by cleaning it from top to bottom and getting new sheets and comforter. When he came home, he was still very swollen and had a good amount of recovery ahead.

Marco's first follow up with the oral surgeon was a week and a half after his surgery. We drove to the doctor's office and were escorted to one of the rooms. Marco took his place in the exam chair, and we waited for the doctor.

The doctor came into the room and began to examine Marco.

I asked, "How is he doing?"

The doctor replied, "He is healing as excellent as any man could."

The nurse came into the room to see if the doctor required any assistance. She took one look at Marco and said, "This is amazing!" then quickly exited, calling to another nurse, "Come and see Marc Fabretti. It's incredible! Did he even have major surgery just a few weeks ago!"

Those words! I was quickly reminded of our prayer and the words that we had asked to hear. They were now ringing in my heart and telling me that the Lord is near. That He indeed does hear and answer the prayers of his people. I was tearing up and looking at Marco to see if he had also made the correlation between what the doctor and nurses had just said and our prayer before surgery.

As we left that office and got into our vehicle to head home, I asked Marco, "Did you hear the words?"

"What words?" he questioned. "The words that were an answer to our prayer, excellent, incredible, amazing! Do you recall our prayer before you went into surgery, asking God to hear these words about your recovery?" I inquired.

Marco responded, "I was really scared that day, but remember how cool it was that the surgical team had assembled around my bed with their head bowed while we were praying."

"Well, then let me remind you that specifically asked our Heavenly Father to hear those three words—excellent, incredible, and amazing to describe your recovery. That prayer was just answered!"

We drove home that day thanking God for the answered prayer!

Dear reader, please know that if you have given your heart to Jesus and are walking in His ways. You don't have to be perfect because frankly, you can't. You have the privilege of praying and being heard.

God's Word tells us, "Confess your faults one to another, and pray one for another, that ye may be healed. The effectual fervent prayer of a righteous man availeth much" (James 5:16).

"For the eyes of the Lord are over the righteous, and his ears are open unto their prayers" (1 Peter 3:12).

Thank you, Lord, for your Word and answered prayer!

CHAPTER 22

The Great Physician

Nearly two decades ago, my mother-in-law, Ellen, was having trouble with her eye. It began to bulge out; she was experiencing double vision and said that she could hear swishing in her ear. She went to her ophthalmologist, who recommended that she see a neuro-ophthalmologist. Based on the referral by her opthalmologist, Ellen was able to secure an appointment very quickly.

I took Ellen to the appointment to take notes and ask questions.

After examination, the neuro-ophthalmologist diagnosed Ellen with carotid-cavernous sinus fistula, which was causing bleeding blood vessels in her brain.

Per the Healthline Newsletter, medically reviewed by George Krucik, MD MBA on January 21, 2016, written by Helen Colledge and Elizabeth Boskey, PhD, a carotid-cavernous sinus fistula (CCF) is an abnormal connection between an artery in your neck and the network of veins at the back of your eye.

These veins at the back of your eye transport blood from your face and brain back to your heart and are located in small spaces behind your eyes called cavernous sinuses. Sometimes an abnormal channel forms between these veins and one of the internal or external carotid arteries that run up each side of your neck.

This formation happens as a result of a small tear that sometimes occurs in one of the carotid arteries. If the tear occurs near the veins in the cavernous sinus, an abnormal channel may form between the artery and the network of veins through which blood may flow. This is called a fistula.

A fistula can raise the pressure in your cavernous sinuses, which may compress the cranial nerves located around the cavernous sinuses. This compression may damage the nerve function, which is to control your eye movements. These cranial nerves also allow you to experience sensation in parts of your face and head. The increased pressure caused by the fistula can also affect the veins that drain your eye. This can cause symptoms such as eye swelling and abnormal vision.

Upon examination, the neuro-ophthalmologist determined that Ellen's condition required immediate attention and called the nurse to see if an operating room would be available in the next few days. There was, and the procedure was scheduled for the next day. Ellen underwent testing to ensure she was a solid candidate for this procedure.

The main type of surgery for CCF is endovascular emboliza-tion. This surgery involves inserting a narrow tube into an artery in your groin. The tube is then threaded up to the fistula. Once there, materials such as metal coils can be used to seal off the connection.

This procedure required Ellen to remain awake on the table although quiet with some medication. I was allowed to sit just out-side the room, and I prayed the entire time. This procedure was slow and concise. Several times, I could hear Ellen's voice that she was getting uncomfortable. The surgeon assured Ellen that she was doing the best she could as expedient as possible. I sat outside and lifted Ellen in prayer asking God to please comfort and quiet her.

After several hours, the surgeon shared with me that she had done the best she could to embolize most but not all of the bleeding blood vessels. I am so very grateful that the Lord was able to quiet Ellen for so long on this operating table while this procedure was in progress. Yes, I know that she was given medicine to quiet her anxiety, but the Lord quieted her heart and calmed her nerves. He whispered to her, "You are my beloved," while she laid on that table. This is why she was so calm and quiet.

Ellen remained in the hospital for a few days to recover, and we went home.

Have you ever experienced the calmness and peace of our God during a difficult time? It may not be surgery. It may be some other storm that entered your life quite unexpectedly. You are suddenly engulfed with the rising waters of bad news. The waves begin to crash against you making you unsteady and overwhelmed. You choose to turn your face toward heaven and cry out to God. Because you are His child, you are confident that He has heard your prayer. Your mind is now flooded with His word.

"So do not fear, for I am with you; do not be dismayed, for I am your God. I will strengthen you and help you; I will uphold you with my righteous right hand" (Isaiah 41:10).

"The Lord is near to all who call on him, to all who call on him in truth" (Psalm 145:18).

"And the peace of God, which transcends all understanding, will guard your hearts and your minds in Christ Jesus" (Philippians 4:7).

Focusing and standing on God's word changes the atmosphere. The circumstances outside of you have not yet changed, however, your perspective has changed. You are now seeing with God's perspective. He has your best in mind, although your emotions may not see it that way, it is truth. Your mind has been redirected to eternity versus just this one single incident or circumstance in your life. You now have a glimpse of the bigger picture. God is in control, and He tells you, His child, not to fear. You are now engulfed by the truth of His word in your life. His word that is alive and active, which is able to pierce the very marrow, the life of your body. His word swirling through your mind and heart, telling your emotions they are no longer dictating. His word that caused the universe to come into existence. His word who brought the dead to life is now taking the lead.

Do not underestimate the power of God's word. Read it, speak it, meditate on it, and memorize it. It will be a deep well of refreshment for your heart and soul. It will bring you peace, rest, and comfort like nothing else can.

Almost a year went by and Ellen began having double vision again and experiencing the same symptoms as before her surgery.

Back to the neuro-ophthalmologist, we went. Once again, the doctor confirmed that Ellen would require surgery. Ellen's second surgery was scheduled for the week of Christmas. Once again, Ellen would need to endure the embolization of bleeding blood vessels in her head. We headed to the hospital and prayed before surgery.

This time, the room I was waiting in was a bit farther from the operating room, and the surgery took much longer. After several hours, the surgeon came out to see me. She shared with me that there are still so many areas that need to be embolized. It has been a long surgery already and is very tedious work. With the holidays so close, she said much of her team is going to be going home. She informed me that this condition is chronic. Ellen will need to have this procedure done on an annual or biannual basis.

I thanked the surgeon for the work she and her team had done thus far. I shared that I deeply appreciated their sacrifice during this Christmas week to be a part of Ellen's surgery. I told the surgeon that I could not possibly tell Ellen that she would need to come back and have this surgery again and certainly not annually. Then I implored her to please pull a team together to embolize as many of the leaks as possible as an incredible surgeon, and I would ask my church to go in prayer to the Great Physician. She agreed. I immediately called the church and put Ellen on the prayer line, then I went to the chapel knelt in prayer and cried out to God like never before. I prayed crying in the Spirit and with understanding.

"In the same way, the Spirit helps us in our weakness. We do not know what we ought to pray for, but the Spirit himself intercedes for us through wordless groans" (Romans 8:26).

I was approached by a few people while I was praying asking if I was okay. I cried so hard and poured out to God my request for Ellen to be healed. I asked Him to please guide the surgeon's hands. The long surgery took a toll on Ellen. In recovery, Ellen was uncomfortable and anxious much of the night. The Lord gave me songs full of scripture to sing over Ellen to comfort her through that night.

"You are my hiding place; you will protect me from trouble and surround me with songs of deliverance" (Psalm 32:7).

The next day, when the family came to visit, Ellen was still very swollen from the surgery and barely recognizable. The next few days and through Christmas, Ellen remained in the hospital, healing from this surgery. The family went to the hospital, and we had Christmas there with Ellen. When she came home, she stayed with family for a little while until the doctor approved her to go home alone.

Time passed. Ellen went for regular check-ups. One year, two years, three years… Almost two decades later, Ellen has not yet had to go back for this surgery. Thank you, Lord, for answered prayer!

There was still irreversible damage with her eye, and she requires a prism in the lens of her glasses to address her double vision, but almost twenty years later, this chronic condition has been healed.

And if there was any doubt…Ellen was having trouble with that eye once again.

An MRI was scheduled, and after the results were read, the doctor determined that scans of Ellen's eye, nearby blood vessels, and cavernous sinus should be reviewed using an angiography to confirm diagnosis.

For an angiography, contrast medium is injected into the blood vessels. Contrast medium is a special substance that shows up on X-rays. An X-ray of your head and neck is then taken. If you have a CCF, it should show up on the image.

We awaited the results. The doctor returned with results. The doctor reported, "This is nothing short of a miracle. There is absolutely no bleeding or leaking."

At those words, my heart was filled with gratitude. Thank you, Lord, for your healing touch I silently whispered to my Heavenly Father.

The doctor continued. I believe Ellen's double vision is a symptom of damage to the sixth nerve. You may notice vision impairment when both eyes are open or when you're looking at something in the distance. Sometimes, double vision occurs when looking in the direction of the damaged eye. This sixth nerve may have been damaged by a TIA, which is a small stroke.

The diplopia or double vision can be corrected by a prism placed in your glasses, which tricks the eye. The doctor sent Ellen to an eye specialist, who ordered the prescription for the prism. As long as Ellen wears these glasses, she is not affected by the double vision.

I am grateful that Ellen had to go back to the doctor and for the doctor ordering the angiography. For this test showed the healing. So if there was any doubt in Ellen's mind that her Heavenly Father touched her and healed her, she could read the results of that test in black-and-white. She could also recall the doctor's words *this is nothing short of a miracle.*

I have found that reason has a tendency to seep into our mind over time. Reasoning of your own understanding or reasoning by well-meaning voices who may not necessarily believe in the God who heals. These voices have a tendency to creep into our mind and perhaps put that miracle on the shelf and replace it with what humanly makes sense.

So this chapter is included in this book to testify of God's amazing power and marvelous works! To ensure that this miracle is spoken of for generations to come!

"He said, 'If you listen carefully to the Lord your God and do what is right in his eyes, if you pay attention to his commands and keep all his decrees, I will not bring on you any of the diseases I brought on the Egyptians, for I am the Lord, who heals you'" (Exodus 15:26).

"See now that I myself am he! There is no god besides me. I put to death and I bring to life, I have wounded and I will heal, and no one can deliver out of my hand" (Deuteronomy 32:39).

"Lord my God, I called to you for help, and you healed me" (Psalm 30:2).

CHAPTER 23

Dust!

When it comes to dust, I am a hater. I could dust on Saturday, and the following day see the evidence of new dust. It settles in so quickly on my mahogany dresser. Before painting my bedroom closet, I found dust on the upper shelf and interior door molding of my bedroom closet! How did it get there?

Dust! More than just dirt, house dust is a mix of sloughed-off skin cells, hair, clothing fibers, bacteria, dust mites, bits of dead bugs, soil particles, pollen, and microscopic specks of plastic according to Google.

I always say…there will be no dust in heaven! 'Cause nothing dead lives there. But what does God's word say about dust?

"Then the Lord God formed a man from the dust of the ground and breathed into his nostrils the breath of life, and the man became a living being" (Genesis 2:7).

"I will make your offspring like the dust of the earth, so that if anyone could count the dust, then your offspring could be counted" (Genesis 13:16).

"Your descendants will be like the dust of the earth, and you will spread out to the west and to the east, to the north and to the south. All peoples on earth will be blessed through you and your offspring" (Genesis 28:14).

Wow! That gives me a whole new view on dust.

Dust was instrumental during the plagues of Egypt.

"Then the Lord said to Moses, 'Tell Aaron, "Stretch out your staff and strike the dust of the ground," and throughout the land of Egypt the dust will become gnats'" (Exodus 8:16).

"Handfuls of soot become fine dust over the whole land of Egypt, and festering boils broke out on the people and animals throughout the land" (Exodus 9:9).

Dust! Used by God in different ways throughout the Bible.

Man was formed *out of the dust*. God breathed life into him…into you…into me. But then, the enemy that wars against our soul came up with a plan to seduce Adam and Eve into handing over what God had given them, and they fell.

So the Lord God said to the serpent, "Because you have done this, Cursed are you above all livestock and all wild animals! You will crawl on your belly and you will eat dust all the days of your life" (Genesis 3:14).

See the contrast? Man was lifted out of and formed from the dust, and God breathed life into him. The serpent…Satan was cast down and cursed to eat the dust. Man has been lifted up out of the dust and the serpent, Satan has been cast down to the dust.

I want to settle here for just a moment. I want to remind each of you who you are. You are God's beloved. He takes great delight in you. He brags on you. He rejoices over you with singing. You are a child of the King, of the Most High God. But Satan would have you think that the best you can do is wallow in the dust…that this is as good as it gets for you…and *you* may have thought that from time to time based on whatever circumstances you found yourself in because life can be hard, and it comes at you fast. You may feel defeated in an area of your life. You may be out of resources, out of strength. Your hope may be teetering on the edge, But we must remember and meditate on what God's Word says…

"He raises the poor from the dust and lifts the needy from the ash heap" (1 Samuel 2:8).

"He knows how we are formed; he remembers that we are dust" (Psalm 103:14).

You see, God is well aware of your circumstances. He is close to the broken hearted. You may feel weighed down by life. Your heart may be heavy and your mind and body tired.

But in the words of Isaiah 52:2: "Shake off your dust; rise up, sit enthroned, Jerusalem. Free yourself from the chains on your neck, Daughter Zion, now a captive."

Whatever may be weighing you down, we are told to throw off.

> Therefore, since we are surrounded by such a great cloud of witnesses, let us throw off everything that hinders, and the sin that so easily entangles. And let us run with perseverance the race marked out for us, fixing our eyes on Jesus, the pioneer and perfecter of faith. For the joy set before him, he endured the cross, scorning its shame, and sat down at the right hand of the throne of God. Consider him who endured such opposition from sinners, so that you will not grow weary and lose heart. (Hebrews 12:1–3)

We are all in this race, and from time to time we can become discouraged. Maybe the dust is kicking up in our face; well-meaning voices may tell us that it is okay to stop and sit out the rest of the race. But let me come alongside you today and remind you of God's word.

"Multitudes who sleep in the dust of the earth will awake: some to everlasting life, others to shame and everlasting contempt" (Daniel 12:2).

"The first man was of the dust of the earth; the second man is of heaven" (1 Corinthians 15:47).

"So the Lord God said to the serpent, "Cursed are you above all livestock and all wild animals! You will crawl on your belly and you will eat dust all the days of your life" (Genesis 3:14).

But the Lord says to His children…

"He delights in those who fear him, who put their hope in his unfailing love" (Psalm 147:11).

"He reached down from on high and took hold of me, he drew me out of deep waters. He rescued me from my powerful enemy, from my foes, who were too strong for me. They confronted me in the day of my disaster, but the Lord was my support. He brought me out into a spacious place; he rescued me because he delighted in me" (2 Samuel 22).

So the next time you see dust and believe me it won't take long, remember that is where you came from, but that is not where you remain. So eat my dust, Satan.

May God's Word encourage you today.

CHAPTER 24

Go and Tell!

Declare his glory among the nations, his
marvelous deeds among all peoples!

—1 Chronicles 16:24 and Psalm 96:3

Sing to the Lord a new song,
for he has done marvelous things!

—Psalm 98:1

These are imperative statements not suggestions.
Life can be challenging, and difficult times can wear on you
and your faith. So before these times hit, prepare yourself.

I encourage you to think upon the goodness of our God and
His marvelous works. He spoke the world into existence in just six
days! He sent a flood to the earth but saved Noah and his family in an
incredible ark. He told Abraham his descendants would be as many
as the stars in the sky and sand at the ocean. He brought the Israelites
out of bondage. He desires to deliver each of us from that same slave
mentality. He sent His Son, Jesus, to earth, who made the lame to
walk, blind to see, and dumb to speak. He healed the sick and raised
the dead!

If you have served the Lord for any amount of time, then you have experienced the marvelous works of the Lord our God. First, you experienced salvation. A new song was placed in your heart, and you became a child of the Most High God. Then through your walk with God, He has answered your prayers. The walls that were built around your heart are slowly crumbling, and your heart is softening toward the Lord.

Write these things down on paper and in your heart and remember them in your head. Remembering these "monumental times" will help when the trials of life threaten to overwhelm, and you are encompassed by darkness. Speak God's Word aloud and declare who He is and all He has done.

Even John the Baptist, Jesus's cousin, needed encouragement at a time when he was in jail. This is the same John who baptized Jesus and saw "the Holy Spirit descend on him in bodily form like a dove. And heard a voice from heaven say to Jesus, 'You are my Son, whom I love, with you, I am well pleased'" (Luke 3:22). Even John needed to be reminded of God's marvelous works.

So John sent two of his disciples to Jesus to ask, "Are you the One or should we look for another?"

John spent his life as a forerunner for Jesus. Yet at this time in his life, the darkness and hard times affected his perception.

"Jesus replied to the messengers, 'Go back and report to John what you have seen and heard: The blind receive sight, the lame walk, those who have leprosy are cleansed, the deaf hear, the dead are raised, and the good news is proclaimed to the poor. Blessed is anyone who does not stumble on account of me'" (Luke 7:22–23).

So Jesus response to John's need was to remind him of the marvelous works of God. When we speak God's Word our spirit man is strengthened.

"Keep this Book of the Law always on your lips; meditate on it day and night, so that you may be careful to do everything written in it. Then you will be prosperous and successful" (Joshua 1:8).

I encourage you to make every effort to meditate continuously on God's Word and His marvelous works. If you know someone who is struggling, remind them of God's marvelous works. For we are living stones fitted jointly together. We need one another. We are running this race together. At times, we get tired or distracted or lose heart and need someone to come alongside and help us keep moving toward the finish line. We need to encourage one another by speaking truth and remind each other what God says. I pray that within the pages of this book you have found hope and help.

"Great and marvelous are your deeds, Lord God Almighty. Just and true are your ways, King of the nations" (Revelations 15:3).

Amen? Amen!

ABOUT THE AUTHOR

Nance has experienced the transforming power of the Word of God and is passionate about sharing it with others. She has taught the Word of God in her church for over thirty years to primaries, teens, and adults. In this book, she shares stories of her life, intertwined with scripture and real-life emotions to which everyone can relate.

At one time, all Nance ever wanted was to know love and to be loved. God demonstrated His love toward her, healed her, made her whole, and has performed so many marvelous works that she cannot keep silent!

Nance's desire is to declare God's marvelous works, "Since our children may not have seen or were too young to remember the times when God answered prayer. Therefore, we need to speak about those times throughout our day, when we lie down and when we get up, when we sit and when we walk along the road. God's works are marvelous! Therefore, we need to tell others about them, especially to the generations that follow."

Nance declares hope within the pages of this book. The hope that comes from knowing the One True God, the God of the scriptures, the Lover of your soul, the One who fights for you. He is alive and well and cares deeply for you. He wants you to know that He has a plan and a purpose for your life. He wants to lead and direct you to bring about a quality of life that you could never experience without Him.

The content of this book showcases that incredible and intimate God who whispers to you in the still of the day, "You are my beloved."